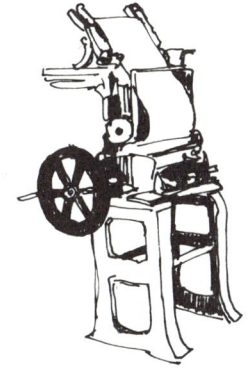

070.4
B46
1980

BEST NEWSPAPER WRITING

1980 Winners

The American Society
of Newspaper Editors
Competition

Edited by
Roy Peter Clark

odern Media Institute
556 Central Avenue
St. Petersburg, Florida 33701

Copyright © 1980 by Modern Media Institute
556 Central Avenue
St. Petersburg, Florida 33701

All rights reserved. No part of this publication may be reproduced or transmitted in any form or by any means, electronic or mechanical, including photocopy, recording, or any information storage and retrieval system, without permission in writing from the publisher.

ISBN 0-935742-02-6
ISSN 0195-895X

Printed in the United States of America

ACKNOWLEDGMENTS

Grateful acknowledgment is made to the following for permission to reprint the newspaper articles included in this book:
The *Washington Post* and Cynthia Gorney for the features which appeared in the *Washington Post*.
The *Providence Journal-Bulletin* and Carol McCabe for the news articles which appeared in the *The Providence Sunday Journal.*
The *Boston Globe* and Ellen Goodman for the essays which appeared in *The Globe*. Copyright © 1979 The Boston Globe Newspaper Co./Washington Post Writers Group.
Modern Media Institute also would like to acknowledge the following for permission to reprint excerpts from the finalists in the American Society of Newspaper Editors Competition:
The *St. Petersburg Times* and Dudley Clendinen.
   Copyright © 1979 The St. Petersburg Times.
The *Philadelphia Daily News* and Pete Dexter.
The *Philadelphia Inquirer* and Richard Ben Cramer.
The *New York Times* and Francis X. Clines.
The *(New York) Daily News* and Michael Daly.
   Copyright © 1979 New York News Inc.
   Reprinted by permission.
The *(Baltimore) News American* and Mark Bowden.
The *Philadelphia Inquirer* and Bill Lyon.
The *Minneapolis Star* and W.D. (Zeke) Wigglesworth.
The *Miami Herald* and Barry Bearak.
The *Los Angeles Times* and Martin Bernheimer.
The *Chicago Sun-Times* and Paul Galloway.
Modern Media Institute also wishes to acknowledge the very special contribution of Marlene Shebu who coordinated the production of this volume.

ABOUT THIS BOOK

It's more than a book, much more. It's an act of generosity by three fine writers and their newspapers, by the American Society of Newspaper Editors (ASNE) and by Roy Peter Clark, the editor of this volume.

They have created something unique, a gift to students, to other writers and to all who love the language and fine writing.

This book represents the final chapter of the 1980 contest sponsored by ASNE to identify and reward outstanding writing in U.S. and Canadian newspapers. It includes the winning entries, Clark's analysis and his perceptive interviews with the writers.

The contest itself is a chapter in ASNE's continuing campaign to give newspaper readers better, more readable writing. It began in 1977 when Clark directed a writing project for the Society, publishing a report, *Writing*, which became a handbook for newspapers throughout the country.

Appearing with a panel of writers at ASNE's 1978 convention, Clark gave editors this prescription: "When a writer comes to a newspaper, he must learn quickly that he is entering an environment in which good writing is encouraged and rewarded."

Another panel member, Steve Lovelady of *The Philadelphia Inquirer*, cautioned that "the reader is looking for an excuse to quit reading at the end of every sentence and every paragraph. Don't give him one."

And William Mathewson of *The Wall Street Journal* added: "The mood and the impact of a piece can depend on how it is worded, not simply on how clear it is and on whether all the relevant facts are presented. But phrasing is taste, and taste, after all, is subjective."

The task of identifying the very best in taste, in rhythm and in overall quality from among more than

625 entries in the 1980 contest was given to the ASNE's Writing and Awards Committee, headed by James K. Batten, vice president for news of Knight-Ridder Newspapers.
Other members were:
Judith W. Brown, *New Britain (Conn.) Herald*
Frank Caperton, *Norfolk Virginian Pilot* and *Ledger-Star*
Edward R. Cony, *Wall Street Journal*
James Hoge, *Chicago Sun-Times*
Maxwell McCrohon, *Chicago Tribune*
C.A. McKnight, ASNE/*Charlotte Observer*
Claude Sitton, *Raleigh News and Observer* and *Times*
William F. Thomas, *Los Angeles Times*
Thomas Winship, *Boston Globe*
John O. Emmerich, Jr., *Greenwood (Miss.) Commonwealth*
Katherine Fanning, *Anchorage News*
A.S. Jones, *Greeneville (Tennessee)Sun*
David Laventhol, *Newsday*
William McIllwain, *Washington Star*
Gene Roberts, *Philadelphia Inquirer*
John Sullivan, *Livingston (Montana) Enterprise*
Fred Taylor, *Wall Street Journal*

The better writing campaign is one on a long list of projects ASNE has undertaken in the 58 years since 75 editors gathered in New York to form a society dedicated to working collectively "for the solution of common problems." And the goal of well-written, readable newspapers may have been on the minds of members when in 1975 they adopted a new statement of principles intended "to preserve and strengthen the bond of trust and respect between American journalists and the American people, a bond that is essential to sustain the grant of freedom entrusted to both by the nation's founders."

This is the second year in which the Modern Media Institute (MMI) has published a book bringing together the contest winners in a single volume. The stories, interviews and analyses make it indispensable to teachers and students, to writers and readers who love good writing. For MMI it is an agreeable project, fitting well into its founding assignment — develop and sponsor unusual programs for media students and professionals.

The Institute was founded in 1975 by the late Nelson Poynter, chairman of the *St. Petersburg Times* and *Congressional Quarterly*. Poynter bequeathed stock in the Times to MMI to fund projects such as this and others including:

Roy Peter Clark's writing seminars for newspaper editors and writers.

Media management courses for newspaper professionals and for graduate students from universities throughout the country.

Two special writing programs for liberal arts students who want to write for publication.

The creation of a modern typographical laboratory where high schools produce prize-winning student newspapers.

Last year the introduction to Volume I of *Best Newspaper Writing* ended this way: "MMI's goals and goals of ASNE in sponsoring competition to identify fine newspaper writing are so closely meshed that some would say this volume was inevitable."

As Volume II goes to press nothing has changed.

Donald K. Baldwin
Director
Modern Media Institute

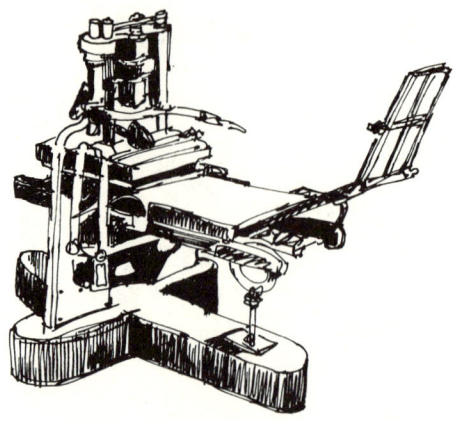

CONTENTS

Introduction / xii

Cynthia Gorney / 3
1980 Prize Winner, Features

Carol McCabe / 65
1980 Prize Winner, News

Ellen Goodman / 123
1980 Prize Winner, Commentary

1980 Finalists / 150

> Dudley Clendinen / 152
> Pete Dexter / 157
> Richard Ben Cramer / 160
> Francis X. Clines / 164
> Michael Daly / 168
> Mark Bowden / 172
> Bill Lyon / 174
> W.D. (Zeke) Wigglesworth / 178
> Barry Bearak / 181
> Martin Bernheimer / 185
> Paul Galloway / 187

INTRODUCTION

Adapted from remarks made to the members of the American Society of Newspaper Editors at the annual convention. April 8, 1980. Washington Hilton, Washington, D.C.

It's been almost two years since I had the opportunity to present my report to you on the writing project at the *St. Petersburg Times*.

I told you then about my intensive one-on-one sessions with reporters, about the critique sheets and seminars designed to create an environment in which good writing is recognized and rewarded.

I also revealed to you my plans to leave the womb of academia for a life of reporting, and let me say that the months that followed that proclamation were the most exhausting of my life. After a year as a so-called writing expert, I was suddenly a writer. My work came under the closest scrutiny from the staff. Each time I sat down to write, I was haunted by a voice. And the voice was my own.

Let me take you back, if I may, to June 4, 1978. I am no longer the writing coach at the *St. Petersburg Times*. I am a reporter now. I have already had two assignments and I've carried them out with vigor and courage. The first was a piece on the new telephone book. The second, a daring report on Daylight Savings Time.

But now I am sitting at my desk in the newsroom, the VDTs thumping pocketa-pocketa-pocketa (I stole the pocketas from Walter Mitty) around me. I dream of great investigative stories. Of exposes. Of Pulitzers.

My city editor approaches.

"OK, Killer, we just heard over the police radio that a car has fallen on a man. Get out there and don't come back without a story."

I speed out to the accident, my car engine roaring pocketa-pocketa-pocketa. I am there for an hour, taking notes, talking to witnesses, family members, paramedics. I return to the office a bit disappointed.

"Whatja get, Killer?"

"Well, Mike, a car did fall on a man, but he's OK. It's not much of a story."

"Whatya mean, a car fell on a man?"

"Yeah, well, the jack slipped and the frame pinned his head to the driveway."

"A car fell on a man's head? How did they get the damn thing off of him?"

"Oh, some teenage boy was walking along the street when he heard this guy scream. He jumped over a fence and past a guard dog and lifted the car off the guy."

I looked across the room at the city editor. I swear I could see his pupils dilating.

I learned a lot that day. I learned that I had no news judgment.

I learned more about writing in four months as a general assignment reporter than in four years of graduate school. I acquired some news judgment. I learned interviewing and reporting techniques. I dealt with the oppressive deadlines and shrinking newsholes, with crabby editors and angry readers.

I've sat bolt upright in the middle of the night, realizing I had made a mistake in my copy. I've picked up the paper on occasion and found that a generous editor had added a grammatical mistake to my story.

Writing for a newspaper was both a great burden and a great joy. I was sent to review a circus that had come into town. I had a 10 o'clock deadline. At 9:30 a brief but frightening fire broke out, momentarily interrupting the show. There was much confusion. An animal broke free but was captured. The fire department was called. My editor said, "You only have 15 minutes, and there's not much room. My first reaction was: No time. No space. What's a writer to do?

But something happened, which I am sure is familiar to all of you, but to me was a revelation. I felt a physiological change, a rush of adrenalin. The limitation of time and space became a challenge. Before I knew it, the story was finished. And I am not ashamed to admit that the next morning I took pleasure in the reading of it.

I also learned of the power of newspaper writing. People cared about what you wrote. I wrote one story and got a call from the governor's office. While covering films, I was wooed by agents and film personalities. Director Robert Altman sat next to me during a preview of one of his films. And I sat ten feet away from Farrah Fawcett when a button on her blouse popped open. Journalism had become a door that gave me access to the rich, the glamorous and the powerful. And this made me uneasy.

I felt better about the local stories I was doing, learning every day of the power of good writing to accomplish good. My story on a polluted body of water got local officials kicking and the Army Corps of Engineers into action. "You got that place cleaned up," my city editor told me.

The telephone company knocked down a building that was being leased as a restaurant by five enterprising young women. Someone who read the story helped them find a new building. "You saved our business," they told me.

The *St. Petersburg Independent* carried a series of stories on hard-to-adopt children. Each story showed a picture of a child, explained candidly but sympathetically the child's history, his or her physical or mental handicaps. Time and again the children would find permanent homes.

So I learned that one reason to write well was that your writing might very well change a person's life.

My greatest lesson as a journalist, and I have incorporated it into my teaching, is the importance of reporting. Without it, there is no good writing. You may have a facility with language. But if you don't have the interesting facts, the details, the quotations, the description, the anecdotes, your writing will have all the substance of a Fanny Farmer nougat.

OK. So you've done the reporting. Now what about the writing? Red Smith once said: "Writing is very easy. All you have to do is sit in front of a typewriter keyboard until little drops of blood appear on your forehead."

Saul Pett put it this way: "Good writing is torment, and anyone who is ashamed of it, who says that torment isn't professional, who cringes from the word *creative* as if it were a horrible tag applied only to queers and poets and not to rough, tough newspapermen, is in the wrong century."

On one of my last days in the *St. Petersburg Times* newsroom, I got a letter from an elderly man. He had read a review I had written, and had underlined a grammatical mistake that I had made. He added the following commentary, which he sent to my editor. "At first I thought the idea of bringing a professor into your newsroom was a great one. Now I'm not so sure." There it was for all to see. A grammatical mistake.

Well, I've kept that letter. I read it often. It teaches me many important lessons. That you can never be scrupulous enough about mechanical accuracy, and that readers aren't stupid.

I have taken part in writing seminars and workshops in 25 states in the last two years. I get letters, phone calls, and visits almost every week from editors dedicated to improving the quality of the writing and editing in their newspapers.

When top editors talk about their agendas for the 1980s, good writing is high on the list. On better writing Tim Hays (editor of *Riverside Press-Enterprise*) said recently: "Too many news stories are hard work for the reader when they don't have to be. The reader doesn't have the time or patience to reread and interpret a muddy lead, let alone a long, muddy story. If there are many of them, he won't write the editor to complain, he'll just drop out."

Accepting the William Allen White award at the University of Kansas, Eugene Patterson (editor of the *St. Petersburg Times*) wondered how White would react to "the graceless ways in which we employ the English language in our contemporary newspapers. White's enduring literary style stands as a rebuke to the carelessness and confusion we inflict on modern readers."

So we hear the call for good writing from editors all over the country.

I believe now in a back-to-basics approach to improving writing. And the basics, as I see them, lie in the relationship between the city editor or features editor and the writer. Between the editor and the writer.

In my travels I have met Charles H. Hamilton, former city editor of the *Richmond News Leader,* editor of a young reporter named James J. Kilpatrick. In those days Kilpatrick was writing long, elaborate and complicated sentences that gnawed on the sensibilities like an impacted wisdom tooth.

One day he received a memo from Charles Hamilton. It had a series of dots across the top. "Those interesting objects are periods. You do not seem to be well acquainted with them. I urge you to try a few. You will find the key that produces them on the bottom row of your typewriter, down toward the right hand end."

The city editor as teacher. What a novel thought. If you want to dramatically improve the quality of the writing in your newspapers, put people in at the assistant city editor level who can work with copy and with writers. That's where the action is.

I'd like to talk to you briefly about the ASNE writing contest and the book *Best Newspaper Writing,* which publishes the winners. The book is a cooperative effort of ASNE and MMI. The 1979 edition contains four groups of stories, with some analysis, and interviews with the writers discussing writing techniques.

This year's volume has the same format but with an added feature. Along with the three winners —Ellen Goodman, Carol McCabe and Cynthia Gorney—we will include samples of the writing of 11 finalists, named by the ASNE judges. Thus, *Best Newspaper Writing 1980* will showcase the work of 14 outstanding newspaper writers. To write well, you must read good writing and that's what this book is about.

Journalism schools have adopted the 1979 book as a text. And wise editors have bought copies for young journalists with very favorable results.

I foresee a great time ahead for newspaper writing. We have purged ourselves of the abuses of the New Journalism: the self-indulgent overwriting, the composite characters, the interior monologues. But we have absorbed into everyday news reporting many of the useful techniques of that movement: setting scenes, using perspective, letting characters speak, using meaningful detail.

Many newspapers are discovering that you can involve the reader in a narrative and still tell the important news high in the story.

Last February, I got a letter from a young woman named Dory Owens, a reporter for the *Billings (Mont.) Gazette*. Dory's editor had handed her a copy of *Best Newspaper Writing 1979*. "I smile with delight," says Dory, "each time I reread the preface you wrote for the book. You have no idea how important and exciting sentences like 'You can be a writer and still work for a newspaper' are to people like me. I believe in the storytelling approach to journalism and want to be very, very good at it." I congratulate Dory's thoughtful editor. There are many young reporters like Dory Owens who are looking for our support and guidance. We cannot let them down. And we cannot let our readers down.

Roy Peter Clark
May, 1980

BEST NEWSPAPER WRITING

Cynthia Gorney

1980 Prize Winner

Features

COMMENTS

Some talented young reporters are making their presence felt on the pages of the nation's top dailies, offering us new directions in newspaper writing, proving day after day that toughminded reporting can be matched with literary grace.

Last year it was Richard Ben Cramer, young foreign correspondent for *The Philadelphia Inquirer*, who impressed the ASNE judges, and more importantly his readers, with dramatic stories of war and peace in the Middle East.

This year's youthful star is Cynthia Gorney. At the age of 26, she is becoming one of the most versatile feature writers in America, as the five stories reprinted here illustrate. She is a tireless researcher and a sensitive interviewer, writing with delicacy, humor, or power, as the situation demands.

Born in Grand Rapids, Michigan, Cynthia Gorney grew up in San Francisco and attended the University of California at Berkeley. After her graduation in 1975, she joined the metropolitan staff of *The Washington Post*. In her own words, she "loved the paper, but hated the town." She returned to San Francisco as a freelancer, but was rehired by *The Post* in 1979. Writing from the West Coast, she is the first person to work for the paper's Style section who was not based in Washington, D.C.

In her person and in her work, she shatters every stereotype of the hard-boiled, detached, unfeeling reporter. She has always had a special interest in disturbed children and the mentally handicapped and for a time taught ice skating to the retarded and a writing course at a mental institution.

She brings the same concern and sensitivity to her reporting. As she reveals in the interview that follows these stories, she sympathizes with the victims she writes about, sharing their grief, and often their tears. Her work proves that this is not weakness.

Cynthia Gorney becomes involved in her stories—hip deep. During the Bicentennial, Gorney was assigned to cover a 35-day bike trip from the Oregon coast to Wyoming. To complete the assignment she biked between 35 and 75 miles per day.

She also loves research, burying herself in books and magazine articles, shuffling through newspaper clips and library card catalogues, before undertaking a delicate interview like the one with Sirhan Sirhan.

While many reporters are wed to superficiality, Gorney divorces herself from it. Whether her story is about frogs, or assassins, or cowboys, or women poker players, or cancer, or doomsday economists, or writers, she learns her topic quickly and with considerable depth. But she is rarely satisfied, always wanting to know more, even when there isn't time.

Gorney loves details, and knows which ones will delight or entice her readers: that the windows in Sirhan's interview room will break into shards or that Dr. Seuss's *There's A Wocket in My Pocket* translates to *Ik heb een Gak in Myn Zak* in the Netherlands.

The details grow into telling anecdotes, such as this one about the perfectionism of Ted Geisel, better known as Dr. Seuss: "In his new book, a volume of tongue twisters coming out in the fall, Geisel has drawn a green parrot. He has studied all the colors on the Random House art department printing chart—his usual procedure—looking for the printer's ink shade that most closely matches his working drawings in colored pencil. There are 60 different shades of green on the chart, and Geisel cannot find the right one. This one is too yellow, that one too red. He does not explain to the art department why green is wrong—just not parrotty enough or something."

Gorney's style for the Dr. Seuss piece is expansive and amusing and slightly worshipful, striking just the right mood for a story on the world famous writer of children's books.

She adopts a much more serious style, straightforward and undecorated, to tell the chilling story of a cancer victim, building a terrifying tempo that concludes with this paragraph's final short sentence: "One of Needham's vaginal tumors was the size of a dime; the second was the size of a nickel. Her vagina, along with the rest of her reproductive system, was surgically removed. She was given an artificial vagina, made from the grafted tissue of her buttocks. She was 20 years old."

Another shift in style gives us the lead to the story of the jumping frogs of Calaveras County, a lead that would have made Grantland Rice or Heywood Broun frog-green with envy: "Willie was a dark frog, in his way; he was young, and exquisitely muscled in the upper leg, where it mattered, but the competition was savage and his jockey was just a kid."

Such good writing is not just magic. It derives from years of reading, natural ability, strong reporting and careful rewriting. In her piece on Sirhan, she wrote the following paragraph over and over, striving for just the right rhythm, balance and meaning: "Does he ever connect that evening, that gun, that one quick lunge and the cry that made close heads turn, *Kennedy, you son of a bitch*—does he link that moment to Richard Nixon's years in office, to Vietnam, to the antiwar movement, to the opening of relations with China, to the first presidential resignation in the nation's history, to the long loud scrape into 1976?"

We should feel encouraged that such a wise and careful sentence should come from such a young reporter.

MAY 20, 1979

ANGELS CAMP, Calif. — Willie was a dark frog, in his way; he was young, and exquisitely muscled, in the upper leg, where it mattered, but the competition was savage and his jockey was just a kid.

At 14 Frank Fasano had as much experience as almost any Angels Camp frog jockey — his uncle, after all, was Frank Borrelli Sr., whose frog broke the world record on that incredible afternoon in 1976 when the record was shattered three times, and young Fasano had won the junior championship twice, once taking it back from his own older brother Bob. But none of that seemed to matter quite so much when you took one look at the lineup:

- Denny Matasci, whose legendary frog E. Davey Croakett practically flew through his required three hops in 1976, besting even Borrelli's frog and setting a new world's record of 20 feet 3 inches, an achievement still emblazoned across the jumping frog jubilee stage.
- Bruce Hamilton, Matasci's young blond protege, who had broken off to form a new frog jockey team of his own and then walked off last year with the jubilee championship.
- Mike Downey, who arrived at Angels Camp with a mobile electric hydromassage frog tank equipped with three thermometers (two of them digital readouts) to insure that the frogs' water maintained a precise C.T.M. — Critical Thermal Maximum.

That was just the beginning. For the entire Oregon Frog Team had come down to Calaveras County, all the way from Sweet Home, Ore., and by Saturday evening their feisty splasher named Marko had already jumped 21 feet 10 inches — not an official record breaker, because only the final jumps count for the record, but still a distance to give a jockey pause. Croaker Jack Jumper, a promising local frog urged on by Calaveras County jockey Vernagac Lee, had jumped an astonishing 22 feet 2 inches in the prelims, raising fervent hopes that Angels Camp might once again regain the world title it lost many years ago to visiting frog jockeys.

And Bill Steed, who had been booted from the Jubilee in 1978 after a frog abuse scandal (he was accused of pressing air out of a frog's thorax to make it stick its legs in the air and grasp a small barbells set, a charge Steed insists was trumped up) qualified two frogs for the finals. M'sieur Jacques, Steed's top qualifier, had reached 17 feet 8 inches on Saturday afternoon — a very respectable jump.

RIBET I

So when Willie's number came up the crowd was still a little restless, full of beer and sunshine, and cheering loudest for the good-natured, shaggy jockeys from Bruce Hamilton's team. Anyway, Willie's preliminary jump had only been an even 17 feet, which is nothing to get really excited about.

Fasano was cool, though.

He walked out on stage with Willie in his hands, gazed briefly at the carpeted jumping area, and then held out his frog, using the popular Matasci-Guzules-Guidici grip, which requires grasping the frog's back with the thumb and forefinger.

Fasano opened his fingers, and Willie dropped to the pad.

Willie looked alert. He arched his back some, with a touch of arrogance — a sure sign, frog jockeys say, that something good is coming. Fasano backed up a little and got ready.

Then Fasano fell to his knees, smashed his hands palm down next to Willie's behind, and screamed, "JUUUUMP!"

Willie jumped. Willie shot into the air, sprang to a graceful landing, and then shot up again, almost before Fasano could scramble in behind him to scream "JUMP!" again. By his third jump, Willie had covered nearly the whole orange carpet — and even as the judges hurried in, stretching their tape measure from his third landing spot to the pad from which he had catapulted, the crowd knew it had seen the best moment of perhaps a great frog. The final measurement was 20 feet 1¼ inches — just an inch and a half short of the record, but long enough to make this handsome seventh grader the youngest frog jockey ever to win the world title.

"Gustine frogs," Fasano's father Eugene declared afterward, referring to the part of the country where Willie had been found, "are the best frogs in the world."

RIBET II

As is by now internationally known, every May Calaveras commemorates the short story written by Samuel Clemens on the basis of some notes he made in the fall of 1865 while staying in the town of Angels Camp. The notes, taken following a mid-billiards-game conversation with an old local, read as follows: "Coleman with his jumping frog bet stranger $50 — stranger had no frog and C got him one — in the meantime stranger filled C's frog full of shot and he couldn't jump. The stranger's frog won."

Clemens, according to the local version of things, thereupon went back to his cabin in Jackass Gulch and wrote, "The Celebrated Jumping Frog of Calaveras County," which made him, so to speak.

These weeks before the 51st Calaveras County Jubilee finals had been frantic: all the frog-box cleaning and preparation, the setting of water temperatures, the dark hours spent wading with a flashlight through the creeks and cattle ditches of northern California in search of healthy frogs. The best of the frog jockeys would say afterward that they worked by instinct as much as anything, squinting at the yellow frog eyes that gleamed in the night like a highway reflector in a headlight glare. Eyes about an inch apart promised good size, somewhere over the 4-inch minimum requirement, but small enough that the frog wouldn't turn out to be

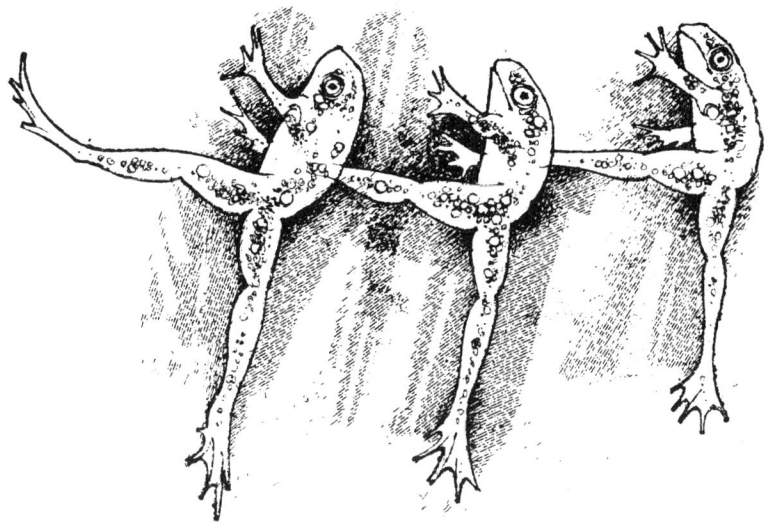

some fat old bullfrog, who could barely shift his bulk off the jumping pad.

It was also necessary, of course, to find frogs without bellyfuls of recently-consumed large meals (whole crayfish are popular, and an experienced frog handler can feel instantly the outline of a crayfish shell in the frog's belly), or eggs. Jumping a pregnant frog would be unkind as well as dumb, and frog safety, particularly in light of the unfortunate Steed incident, was paramount at the jubilee this year.

The public frogs, the ones brought in en masse by the Angels Camp Boosters for temporary loan to novice jockeys-sans-frog, were protected by a much-heralded Frog Safety System, which was demonstrated at a press conference six days before the finals. The system's bulwark was a set of six frog-holding tanks (two of them named, respectively, after the great E. Davy Croakett and another particularly well-liked frog, Man O'Warts) and two rest and relaxation tanks, all surrounded by wire mesh, and guarded by a security patrol. It was hoped that this would prevent overjumping, frog tampering, drugging and any other form of abuse that might cast a pall over the competition.

RIBET III

The private frogs rested in individual compartmentalized sliding-top frog boxes, each protected primarily by a stern set of written regulations and an implicit code of honor among the veteran jockeys. "I have not eaten a frog leg in my life." Mike Downey, who is generally a carpet sales vice-president from Concord, Calif., said with some asperity, "I don't intend to. Be like eating your dog."

The Downey hydromassage unit was an innovation, and the source of some rumor and interest; Downey himself, after a disappointing final showing, decided he would add a power air vent to the unit and try it again next year.

But if he intended to change his Critical Thermal Maximum, Downey would not let on. Frog temperature is thought by many jockeys to be the key to a great jump since frogs become lethargic when they're too hot and start hibernating when they're too cold. It is also a closely guarded secret. "It's a very critical temperature you get to," Downey said.

He had logged, in a red plastic binder, the precise personal data of every frog jumped by the Downey group for the 17 years they have attended the jubilee: Castor Bean, Clusterberry, Cotton Top, Bee Flood, Fuzzy Tongue, all logged in by sex, size, weight, water temperature and jump distance.

It was more than just C.T.M. that separated the fine jockeys on Sunday though — it was technique, the jockeying skill that is so much a by-product of experience. Tom Beatty, a Visalia, Calif., restaurant owner (whose great hope called Snort did a smashing 18 feet 11 inches in the prelims but then pooped out), said he favors the feet-first scare technique, in which the jockey stomps the stage to either side of the frog's behind while shouting some terrible shout, much like a samurai preparing for battle. This has the advantage of quick recovery, allowing the jockey to spring forward and scare the frog into its second jump, but there is always the danger that the jockey will find himself standing right over the frog, thus confusing him.

"That happened with Bandit I," Beatty said. Bandit I had gone 16 feet 3 inches on his first two jumps, but on the third Beatty landed wrong and the frog, alarmed, hopped off to the side. "I over-jockied him," Beatty said.

Once in a long while a jockey using the feet-first scare technique will also find himself landing on the frog, but that is quite tragic and rare and it is best not to think about it.

RIBET IV

The Oregon frog team, which presented a formidable threat in the preliminaries but suffered some awful blows toward the end, used the unusual hindlegs frog drop they are credited with having introduced to Calaveras county (the jockey swings the frog by its legs onto the pad), and added interest by crouching behind certain hesitant frogs and blowing vigorously on their hindquarters.

"So far as I'm concerned," said John Hand, the grass-seed buyer who coaches and leads the Oregon team (its members are primarily his immediate family), "Matasci's the all-round guy to beat. He's got good frogs. We've learned a lot from him. He's learned a lot from us. But I think we've got some really good frogs."

There were a small number of frog fatalities, due to drownings, overexhaustion and accidental trauma. It was understood that these frogs would be put quietly to rest. The jockeys, for their part, agreed that as usual they would release their frogs back into the wild — although the Matascis said their best jumpers would be placed in a certain hidden pond, a frog stud pond, if you will, where E. Davy Croakett was taken to produce more champions like himself.

Willie, according to his jockey, will probably be returned to a frog swamp much like the one from which he came.

FINAL RESULTS

Senior Open Jump: 1. Willie, Frank Fasano, 20' 1¼"; 2. Santa Marta Gold, Douglas Yorke, 18' 8"; 3. Chip, Bob Fasano, 18' 6¼"; 4. Big Jumper, Kathy Campo, 18' 3½"; 5. E. Waterbug, Marc J.Guibdogici, 17' 11½"; 6. Nipples, Brent Bloom, 17' 10½"; 7. Gringo, Arthur Rose, 17' 8¼"; 8. Happy Harry, Bill Steed, 17' 8".

Governors' Jump: 1. Slats, Gov. Robert List of Nevada, 18' 7¾"; 2. No. 1, Gov. Charles Thone of Nebraska, 16' 2"; 3. Phantom's Jug-of-Rum, Gov. John Dalton of Virginia, 15' 5"; 4. Curb's Cuties, Lt. Gov. Mike Curb of California, 15' 1"; 5. (unknown), 13' 4½"; 6. Rebate, Gov. James Hunt of North Carolina, 12' 7"; 7. Happy Hopper, Gov. Victor Atiyeh of Oregon, 12' 5½".

Assemblymen's Jump: 1. Fisherman's Folly, Ted Bugas of Washington, 15' 2"; 2. Jim Kelly's Nugget, Karen Mays of Nevada, 13' 4¼"; 3. Palace Club, Paul May of Nevada, 13' 3¼"; 4. Three's Kinky, Hardy Myers of Oregon, 11' 3½"; 5. T. C., Mae Yih of Oregon, 10' 4½"; 6. Pepsi Day, Sue Wagner of Nevada, 10' 3¼"; 7. Banzai Bannai, Assemblyman Bannai of Nevada, 9' 10¾"; 8. Starlight, Assemblyman Byers of Oregon, 8' 5¼".

Media Jump: 1. Hoppin' Bob, Albany Democrat-Herald of Oregon, 21' 10"; 2. Occupation — Bum, KYLO Davis, 18' 7¾"; 3. Deadline, Charlie Amador (L.A. Press Club), 17' 9½"; 4. Liberty 2, United Ireland Press, 15' 10"; 5. Pepsi Day, KOH Nevada, 15' 2½"; 6. Arthur Frogfrey, KLIV San Jose, 14' 8¾"; 7. Liberty 1, Irish Weekly, 14' 8½"; 8. Jumpin' Machine, KIOI San Francisco, 14' 6½".

MAY 21, 1979

LA JOLLA, Calif. — One afternoon in 1957, as he bent over the big drawing board in his California studio, Theodor Seuss Geisel found himself drawing a turtle.

He was not sure why.

He drew another turtle and saw that it was underneath the first turtle, holding him up.

He drew another, and another, until he had an enormous pileup of turtles, each standing on the back of the turtle below it and hanging its turtle head, looking pained.

Geisel looked at his turtle pile. He asked himself, not unreasonably, What does this mean? Who is the turtle on top?

Then he understood that the turtle on top was Adolf Hitler.

"I couldn't draw Hitler as a turtle," Geisel says, now hunched over the same drawing board, making pencil scribbles of the original Yertle the Turtle drawings as he remembers them. "So I drew him as King What-ever-his-name-was, King" (scribble) "of the Pond." (Scribble.) "He wanted to be king as far as he could see. So he kept piling them up. He conquered Central Europe and France, and there it was."

(Scribble.)

"Then I had this great pileup, and I said, 'How do you get rid of this impostor?'

"Believe it or not, I said, 'The voice of the people.' I said, 'Well, I'll just simply have the guy on the bottom burp.'"

Geisel looks up from his drawing board and smiles — just a little, because a man is taking his picture and he has never gotten used to people who want to take his picture.

Dr. Seuss, American institution, wild orchestrator of plausible nonsense, booster of things that matter (like fair play, kindness, Drum-Tummied Snumms, Hooded Koopfers, and infinite winding spools of birthday hot dogs), detractor of things that don't (like bullying, snobbery, condescension, gravity and walls), is 75 years old this year.

As usual, he is somewhat embarrassed by all the fuss.

"It's getting awful," Geisel says, "because I meet old, old people, who can scarcely walk, and they say, 'I was brought up on your books.' It's an awful shock."

There is probably not a single children's book author in America who has matched the impact, popularity and international fame of the spare, bearded California prodigy who signs his books Dr. Seuss.

Since 1936, when Ted Geisel the advertising illustrator first wrote *And to Think That I Saw It on Mulberry Street,* his books have sold 80 million copies in this country alone.

Mulberry Street was an effort, he explained later, to expel from his brain the maddening rhythm of a ship engine he had heard during the whole of a transatlantic voyage (da da Da da da Da da da Da da da da).

The late Bennett Cerf — at a time when his Random House writers included William Faulkner and John O'Hara — is on record as having called Geisel the only genius of the lot.

The drawings, manuscripts, and half-formed doodles of Dr. Seuss (who did not officially become a doctor until 1956, when Dartmouth College made him an honorary Dr. of Humane Letters), are kept in locked stacks of the Special Collections division of the UCLA library. He won two Academy Awards for his World War II-era documentary film and one for the cartoon "Gerald McBoing-Boing," which he created. His books are published in about 45 countries outside the United States, including Brazil, Japan, the entire British commonwealth and the Netherlands, where *There's A Wocket in My Pocket* translates to *Ik heb een Gak in Myn Zak!*

On his last visit to Australia, his plane was met by reporters, television cameras, person-sized Cats In Hats, small children with "I love you, Dr. Seuss" badges, and a newspaper headline that read "Dr. Seuss Is Here." An official in the Afghan embassy sent him a collection of brilliant blue sculpted animals with mysterious shapes and corkscrew necks, all made according to traditional design in a tiny Afghanistan town whose name Geisel could never pronounce, but which he says has been unofficially renamed Seussville. "Somebody discovered they were stealing my stuff 3,000 years ago," Geisel says, gazing down admiringly at a small sort of yak. "They're pretty good Seuss, though."

Geisel has lived for 30 years in La Jolla, which is a coastal town just north of San Diego that has developed a flowery, almost Caribbean sparkle as the wealthy build homes up the side of the mountain. At the very top of one of the mountains, with the diminishing acres of wild land to the east and to the west the wide blue curve of the Pacific, Geisel and his wife Audrey share an old stucco observatory tower and the elegant, helter-skelter maze of rooms they have built around it. "It just grew," Audrey Geisel said, "Seuss-like."

They have a swimming pool, a small Yorkshire terrier whose front end is indistinguishable from the back at first glance ("I've been accused of having drawn him," Geisel says), and a gray Cadillac Seville with GRINCH license plates — which took them several years to obtain, because when they first applied they learned that an ardent Seuss-lover with four children had already put GRINCH on the license plates and both sides of his RV. He finally moved to Iowa City and released GRINCH back to the Geisels, with a note of apology for having hogged it so long.

San Diego children know Dr. Seuss lives in a white castle on the hill, and on occasion they will pack up peanut butter and jelly sandwiches and set out for the summit, seeking an audience. Mrs. Geisel has come to expect this. "Breathing on the intercom," she calls it. Geisel has no children of his own (Mrs. Geisel, whom he married 12 years ago after the death of his first wife, has two from a previous marriage), and although he is almost always polite to his callers, the sheer numbers of intercom breathers sometimes overwhelm him.

He cannot answer all his letters, either, because they come every month by the hundreds to his home and the Random House offices in New

York — love letters, valentines, air letters from India and New Zealand, photographs of cakes decorated with Hippoheimers or Loraxes, various homemade varieties of Oobleck, the nasty green slime that rains on Bartholomew Cubbins; and in one dismaying delivery, Geisel says, a carefully wrapped package of green eggs and ham.

"These days I spend my birthday in Las Vegas," Geisel says, with unconvincing grumpiness. "Nobody will look for a children's book author in Las Vegas."

He is a private, engaging, intensely driven man, with a lean and sharp-nosed look that gives him an air of severity at first. His house is scattered with his own paintings and busts of creatures unlike anything anybody ever saw before, and as he leads visitors through the halls he makes congenial introductions, as though presenting boarders: "This is a green cat in the Uleaborg, Finland subway ... this is a cat who was born on the wrong side of town ... this is my religious period. This is Archbishop Katz ... this is called, 'Good god, do I look as old as all that?' "

He will not wear conventional neckties — only bow ties. He reads paperback books — history, biography, detective novels — so voraciously that his wife makes regular bookstore runs (often to a certain store that saves new books for him in a special Geisel cubbyhole) and then stashes the paperbacks away so she can hand him new ones in the evening, one at a time. He reads for distraction. He needs it. When he is at work, the names, the verse, the story line, the colors, the shapes and sizes of his extraordinary characters all press upon him. He tapes the working drawings to the wall and stares at them, rearranging, reading aloud to himself, feeling the rhythm of the words.

In his new book, a volume of tongue twisters coming out in the fall, Geisel has drawn a green parrot. He has studied all the colors on the Random House art department printing chart

— his usual procedure — looking for the printer's ink shade that most closely matches his working drawings in colored pencil. There are 60 different shades of green on the chart, and Geisel cannot find the right one. This one is too yellow, that one too red. He does not explain to the art department why each green is wrong — just not parrotty enough, or something.

They know better than to ask. They will have the printer make up the precise shade of green.

"His color sense," says Grace Clarke, executive art director of the Random House junior books division, "is the most sophisticated I've ever run into." Geisel had to completely relearn color during the last two years, after undergoing an operation for removal of a cataract. The right saw brilliant color, following the operation: "the other eye, which still has a small cataract, sees everything like Whistler's Mother." The second cataract is to be removed next year, after which, says Geisel, deadpanned, "They claim I'll be as good as Picasso."

Geisel does not read childrens' literature, unless he is editing it, which is part of his job as the founder and head of the special early readers Random House Division called Beginner Books. Then he is fierce in his judgment, dismissing instantly the noxious breed of childrens' books that coo and mince and pat little heads.

"Bunny-bunny books," he calls them. "Sugar plums, treacle, whimsy." He once turned down a manuscript from Truman Capote. (Diplomatically, neither Geisel nor the Random House people remember what it was about.) "I try to treat the child as an equal," Geisel has said, "and go on the assumption that a child can understand anything that is read to him if the writer takes care to state it clearly and simply enough."

There is a vast difference, of course, between respectful simplicity and invention, and Geisel is as mystified about that as anybody —

about what makes one man dull a ship engine's throb with aspirin, or neat whiskey, while another hears the beginnings of an imaginary backstreet elephant-and-giraffe parade. Geisel never set out to be a children's book writer. He was born in Springfield, Mass., the son of a German immigrant who had been, at various times, a brewer, a park superintendent, and a world champion rifle shot. Ted Geisel grew up in Springfield, graduated from Dartmouth, and spent a year at Oxford, during which time he is reported to have proposed (unsuccessfully) a new edition of *Paradise Lost,* which would include such illustrations as the Archanged Uriel sliding down a sunbeam with an oil can to lubricate his trip.

He lived in New York, selling drawings, stories and political cartoons to magazines of the day — *Judge, Vanity Fair,* the *Saturday Evening Post* — and for 15 years he worked in advertising for Standard Oil of New Jersey.

He drew insecticide ads, "Quick, Henry! The Flit!" That was Geisel's creation.

He illustrated two volumes of jokes, tried unsuccessfully to sell an alphabet book, and then in 1936 laid out the wonderfully paced mad fantasy of the boy named Marco in *And To Think That I Saw It On Mulberry Street*. Before a publishing friend of Geisel's took the book in at Vanguard Press, 20 publishers turned it down.

He had an easier time with the next one. "I was sitting in a railroad train, going up somewhere in Connecticut," Geisel says. "And there was a fellow sitting ahead of me, who I didn't like. I didn't know who he was. He had a real ridiculous Wall Street broker's hat on, very stuffy, on this commuting train. And I just began playing around with the idea of what his reaction would be if I took his hat off and threw it out the window."

Geisel smiles a small, slightly evil smile.

"And I said, 'He'd probably just grow another one and ignore me.'"

Which gave us *The 500 Hats of Bartholomew Cubbins*. Boy, confronted in castle by snooty royalty, cannot doff his hat because new hats keep appearing to replace it.

"In those days 90 percent of the stuff that was written was literary fairy tales," Geisel says. "I began to think of appurtenances around the castle, and one of them would be a bowman, and then it occurred to me there would also be an executioner. And I said, 'We gotta get a little bastard of a crowned prince in here.' And I would draw and semi-write that sequence up. Then I would put it on the wall and see how they fit. I'm not a consecutive writer."

Once in a while there is an echo of something like anguish in Geisel's accounts of the workings of his own imagination — some constant, furious homage to the 1902 rifle target, its bullseye perforated by his father's exacting shots, that Geisel keeps mounted on the wall.

"To remind me of perfection," he says.

He will sometimes work late into the night, or break off into an entirely different project, when some flaw in a book begins to gnaw at him. He spent a full year struggling over the smallish gopher-like creature called the Lorax. "Once he was mechanized. That didn't work. He was big at one point. I did the obvious thing of making him green, shrinking him, growing him."

And then? "I looked at him, and he looked like a Lorax."

But he was equally stumped by the story itself, a dismal tale about the Once-ler, who hacks down all the Truffula Trees to mass-produce Thneeds, thereby driving away the Swomee-Swans, starving out the Brown Bar-ba-loots, and — as the wheezing, outraged Lorax cries — "glumping the pond where the Humming-fish hummed." It was the angriest story Geisel had ever written, and he could not figure out how to make sense of it, how to keep it from turning into a lecture — a preachment," as Geisel says. Geisel has a horror of preachments. Audrey Geisel, who quite rightly believes that the best way to come unstuck is to stand on your head and try looking at things that way, suggested they go to Africa for a while, which they did.

"I hadn't thought of the Lorax for three weeks," Geisel says. "And a herd of elephants came across the hill — about a half mile away — one of those lucky things, that never happened since. And I picked up a laundry pad and wrote the whole book that afternoon on a laundry pad." The final version of *The Lorax* still begins in its ominous, haunting way:

At the far end of town
Where the Grickle-grass grows
And the wind smells slow-and-sour when it blows.
And no birds ever sing excepting old crows . . .
Is the street of the Lifted Lorax.

But it ends with some hope. One Truffula-Tree seed makes it through. And that, for Geisel, redeems the preachment. Happy endings, he has said, are vital: "A child identifies with the hero, and it is a personal tragedy to him when things don't come out all right."

Geisel, in an early fit of misguided inspiration, once wrote a book for adults. "My greatest failure," he says, pulling a rare copy off the bookshelf. "This is a book that nobody bought."

Its thesis is that there were in fact seven Lady Godivas (Gussie, Hedwig, Lulu, Teenie, Mitzi, Arabella, and Doreas J.), each of them engaged to one of the seven Peeping Brothers. In order to avenge the unfortunate death of their father, who was tossed by an arrogant horse enroute to the Battle of Hastings, the Ladies Godiva set out to discover Horse Truths (don't look a gift horse in the mouth, and so on) while displaying limited but alluring portions of their anatomies.

"I don't think I drew proper naked ladies," Geisel says sadly. "I think their ankles came out wrong, and things like that." The book was published in 1937, priced steeply during the depression at $2 a copy, and less than a quarter of the 10,000 sold. They now go for $100 to $200. Geisel has a private fantasy about making the Godivas into an animated film, but he is not certain about how to present nudity — the ankles, and things like that.

But the bulk of Geisel's audience will always be children. "Writing for adults doesn't really interest me anymore," he said. "I think I've found the form in writing for kids, with which I can say everything I have to say a little more distinctly than if I had to put it in adult prose."

He pulls from a file some typewritten pages from his new book, "You want to try reading one?" Geisel asks.

His visitor, reading slowly, makes a stab at it:

*One year we had a Christmas brunch
With Merry Christmas Mush to munch.
But I don't think you'd care for such
We didn't like to munch mush much.*

There is a rather bad moment of tongue-twisting at the end and Geisel looks delighted. "These things are written way over the ability of first grade kids, and I think it's going to work," he said. "They're stinkers (the tongue-twisters, not the children).

"I think one reason kids are not reading up to their potential is a lack of being urged — you can't urge them with a big stick, but you can urge them with competition."

Well now, demands his visitor, Geisel has to read one.

"Not wearing the right glasses," Geisel says quickly. "I can't."

AUGUST 20, 1979

First of two parts

"He would be a grandfather.

"He would have finished his two terms as president and at 53, Robert Kennedy would be devoting a good part of his time to his family. The absence of day-to-day pressures would enable him to go with the young children, one by one, on the kinds of educational trips he took as a young man – with Justice Douglas to Russia and alone to the Middle East in 1948.

"He would still be a public man. He would be available for difficult diplomatic missions on special assignment – a young Averell Harriman. He would be a force of conscience – refusing to let us ignore the poor. He'd be pressing women's issues. . . . He'd be organizing the effort to break the OPEC cartel.

"He would not be practicing law – he would not *be teaching – he would* not *be a senator or a congressman, nor a governor nor a Supreme Court justice. He couldn't sit still long enough, even at 53. In short, he'd still be Robert Kennedy, and I still miss him."*
—Joe Dolan, Robert Kennedy's administrative assistant 1965-68.

SOLEDAD, Calif. — He speaks of Christianity, of Rosalynn Carter, of reverence for human life, of the Magna Carta, of God. He speaks several times of God. His eyes, large and dark, keep watching for reaction: It has been 10 years since he sat before a woman who was not a prison official or his mother. "Do you understand me?" His voice is anxious. "Am I relating to you?"

His hair is thick, black and wavy; his skin the color of untreated leather. Short, deep lines furrow down from either side of his nose. He is a small man, hard in the shoulders and arms, and the smile now is spreading wide across his face.

"I have made my peace with myself, ma'am" he says. "And with my God. And I've indicated my desire to make my peace with the whole of humanity. Even those Jews."

Sirhan Bishara Sirhan, age 35, Prisoner B21014, State Correctional Training Facility, Soledad, has taken the end seat at the conference table in PHU 1, the maximum security area where he has spent the last seven years. The letters stand for Protective Housing Unit, which is the State of California's way of saying that Sirhan is in semi-isolation; he and 124 other prisoners of varying notoriety spend their days moving on schedule between single-bed cells, a barred and narrow commons area, and a small recreation yard where they remain, segregated from the rest of the prison. Sirhan's fellow PHU 1 inmates have included one of the men who kidnaped and buried a school bus full of children in Chowchilla, Calif., and Juan Corona, who was convicted of murdering 25 farm workers and burying their multilated bodies in the Feather River Valley. Sirhan's cell is on the third tier of the unit. Eight locked doors, including one barred gate that can be opened only by two officers turning keys simultaneously, separate the cell from the outside world.

"A routine of monotony," Sirhan says. "Period. You just wake up in the morning; they feed you; you have a lockup. One side of the building comes out one day and another side comes out another day.... You feel like a Pavlovian animal." The heavy midmorning light of the Salinas Valley comes through the conference room window. The window is barred. The pane is tattersalled with lead, so that even if shattered the glass would cling in place in shards. Sirhan wears a white T-shirt, blue jeans and a solid prison-issue belt around his narrow waist.

He says he did not eat breakfast.

He says he was too nervous to eat.

He says he would like to make it known that he is remorseful, that he believes it was wrong to have killed another human being, that he feels sorrow at having murdered a father and husband.

He also says he has been in prison long enough. Sirhan Sirhan, who wrenched aside the 1970s with the force that history gives only to political assassins, wants to go home.

California Democratic primary. Los Angeles, 1968. The time comes back in shredded nightmare: the crowded ballroom at the Ambassador Hotel, the elated candidate, the noisy crush of friends and reporters. "I want to express my gratitude," said the candidate, smiling into the crowd, "to my dog Freckles."

It was just past midnight, June 5. Robert Francis Kennedy, the New York senator with the soaring hopes and the thick brown hair falling over his forehead, had just pulled 198 California delegates and 46 percent of the popular vote. "I think we can end the divisions within the United States," Kennedy said, ". . . the violence, the disenchantment with our society . . . .

We are a great country, an unselfish country and a compassionate country. I intend to make that my basis for running." Then he stepped away from the speaker's platform, through a gold curtain, and into the stainless steel-lined serving kitchen where Sirhan Sirhan shot him to death.

The assassin was a thin little blur — burnished skin, black disheveled curls. He shouted: "Kennedy, you son of a bitch!" He pointed a small black .22 caliber revolver at Kennedy's head, and fired, and Kennedy went down, and the expression on Sirhan's face bore into the memory of at least one witness: "A very sick-looking smile."

"Let me explain!" Sirhan screamed afterward, as football player Roosevelt Grier and Olympic star Rafer Johnson hurled their huge bodies onto his, holding him down, shielding him from the crowd. "I can explain," Sirhan cried. "I did it for my country. I love my country." Robert Kennedy's head bled out into the pantry. For a long time afterward — after he had been pronounced dead at Good Samaritan Hospital, and the New York City mourners had waited all night outside St. Patrick's Cathedral for a glimpse of his funeral, and the slow train south had carried his body past weeping crowds down to Arlington Cemetery, and his coffin had been lowered by candlelight into the earth near the grave of his murdered older brother — long after all that was over, it was the dying that clung to memory, the picture of the presidential candidate bleeding to death on a Los Angeles kitchen floor.

Sirhan was identified within hours as a Christian Palestinian Arab, but many Americans were not entirely sure, 11 years ago in the historically pro-Israel United States, what that meant. June 5 was the first anniversary of the Six-Day War, in which Israel took the Sinai, the Golan heights and East Jerusalem. Palestinian guerrillas had not yet attracted much American attention, and most of the nation shared a profound ignorance of the political time bomb that was The Palestinian Problem.

In the following weeks, and especially during the trial, Sirhan's cry of "I did it for my country" became clearer: Robert Kennedy, a firm supporter of Israel who had just reiterated his proposal that 50 Phantom jets be sent to the Israelis, had been murdered by a Jerusalem-born Arab who had apparently spent much of his childhood watching the violence that ultimately expelled many Palestinians from the new nation of Israel.

CONTRASTING PICTURES

He trains with weights. He can press 300 pounds, but he is uneasy about making that known, because he says people will think he is big and mean. "That's the public image of me, the impression of me, is that I'm a very big monster person, as if I'm a big ghoul of some sort. And when they look at me and see my size . . . it baffles them. The facts do not fit the propaganda."

The smile again: quick, hesitant, uncertain. He seemed anxious at first, stiff and awkward in his hard-backed chair; now he leans forward on his elbows, hungry for audience. "Relax," he says softly, as though savoring the interview. "You're too quick."

He has been described, in the years since June 1968, in wildly contrasting ways.

He has been described as a paranoid schizophrenic — who sought inner knowledge from mail-order Rosicrucian texts, who hypnotized himself in the bathroom mirror until at one point Robert Kennedy's face flickered in to replace his own, who wrote unevenly into private notebooks, over and over.

RFK must be
be be disposed of
d d d
disposed of
disposed of openly
Robert Fitzgerald
Kennedy must soon die
die die die die
die die die die die
My determination to eliminate RFK is becoming more the more of an unshakeable obsession

He has been described as a cold political assassin, practicing at the target range all day before the shooting, carrying a loaded gun to the Ambassador Hotel, asking several times whether Kennedy would pass through the pantry.

"Sirhan is saner than you or me," Carmen Falzone, a former Soledad convict who said he had spent time with Sirhan in PHU 1, told a *Playboy* interviewer last year. "He told me he made up all that trance and hypnosis stuff . . . He told me the love for the Kennedys was declining, so now he wanted to make himself look more sympathetic in the media . . . I found out

Sirhan was highly intelligent, one-directional, emotionless, and suspicious, the perfect terrorist."

And finally he has been discribed as a quiet boy, a bookish boy, a lonely foreigner, traumatized in childhood and pushed finally into obsessional madness by the discovery that the senator he admired was a long time supporter of Israel. His mother still lets loose with the litany of horrors she says the boy Sirhan witnessed in Jerusalem 30 years ago: the soldier blown apart by dynamite, his dismembered leg hanging off the bell tower of the Anglican church; the severed hand that floated up in the bucket Sirhan had just dipped into a well; the army truck, swerving away from gunfire, that struck and killed Sirhan's older brother.

"It breaks my heart. I nearly died in those days, it breaks my heart," Mary Sirhan says, on the telephone from her home in Pasadena. "He can't help it." She says he signs his letters to her with a blessing in Arabic: *God is able, and his hand never gets short.*

"I don't think of myself as a killer," Sirhan says. "I'm just a human being, like everybody else. The whole idea of killing people is so offensive to me, it's so alien to everything I've been brought up with, and my values . . . it's hard for me to recognize it as an event even — not even being aware of actually pulling out a gun and aiming it at another human being and pumping away. It's contrary to my upbringing as a Christian."

It has been stipulated, as one of the conditions for this interview, that Sirhan Sirhan will not be asked in detail about the shooting, the days that led up to it, or the various conspiracy theories that some poeple believe have never been adequately explored. (Most of those theories center around controversial ballistics testing that led some observers to conclude that a second gun must have been used in the murder.)

NO MEMORIES

He says only, as he has in the past, that he cannot remember the shooting.

He says he cannot remember any gathering hate toward Robert Kennedy, cannot remember planning his act.

"In fact I was a supporter of [Robert] Kennedy. I was an admirer. That great exhortation of the president — 'ask not what you can do for your country' — I think that had quite an impact on my mind."

He says he only dimly remembers having seen the May 1968 television documentary about Robert Kennedy that was said to have outraged Sirhan with its delineation of Kennedy's admiration for Israel.

Does he remember the notebooks? "No." A sympathetic smile. "The greatest regrets."

He says the evidence and testimony at his trial showed that when he shot Kennedy he was in a trance, drunk on four Tom Collinses, and overwhelmed by the noise and bright lights. "I must have been beside myself," he says. "They say I'm lying, and all that. Well, damn it, if you don't want to believe it, don't. But that is the cold fact."

On April 23, 1969, after a jury had convicted him of first degree murder, Sirhan Sirhan was sentenced to die in the gas chamber at San Quentin prison. He stayed on death row for two years, nine months and 26 days until the California Supreme Court struck down the death penalty as cruel and unusual punishment; California voters later restored capital punishment, but Sirhan, like the other prisoners on death row at the time of the court decision, was permanently reprieved. He was transferred to Soledad, which sits like a row of great white dice amid the vineyards and lettuce fields, about 120 miles south of San Francisco.

He reads Arabic journals in his cell: *Al Ahram,* a daily Egyptian newspaper; *Falastine Al-Muhtelhe,* the official organ of the PLO (The name means "Occupied Palestine"). He listens to classical music on the radio, and talk shows — he likes the sound of voices. He loves the great

Arabic alto Umm Kuthum, who used to sing rich, slow, two-hour laments of religious fervor and unrequited love, but he has not had a record player since he left death row. A departing prisoner at Soledad gave him a portable black-and-white television, which had been broken for about eight months; before it broke, Sirhan says, he used to watch a lot of public television, especially the English dramas. He liked "I, Claudius" and "Upstairs, Downstairs." "The Forsythe Saga" was his favorite.

"They have me going to college, as they call it here," Sirhan says, with a hint of mockery in the word *college*. He has already studied oceanography, business economics and social science 139, entitled "Molding American Values." He is currently taking cultural geography and an anthropology class specializing in Mexico. The subject of Israel was raised in his cultural geography class. "Superficially," Sirhan says. "I abstained (from) any involvement in that discussion." He smiles. "It was very heated."

Sirhan Sirhan was 24 years old, three years over what was then voting age, when he murdered the man who might have been president of the United States. It took him less than 30 seconds, and a second hand revolver that retailed for $31.95. Does he think about the presidency, in the walled-in quiet of his California prison cell?

Does he ever connect that evening, that gun, that one quick lunge and the cry that made close heads turn, *Kennedy, you son of a bitch* — does he link that moment to Richard Nixon's years in office, to Vietnam, to the antiwar movement, to the opening of relations with China, to the first presidential resignation in the nation's history, to the long loud scrape into 1976?

"To paraphrase Jesse Unruh, who opposed the establishment of my parole date," Sirhan says, "he was saying that if Sirhan did not kill Robert Kennedy, we would not have had Watergate."

'I KILLED THE PRESIDENT'

He is quoted on this matter in the *Playboy* piece. "I asked Sirhan," Falzone told his interviewer, " 'If you were angry because the U.S. supported Israel, why didn't you kill the president, kill LBJ?' He started to tremble, those dark eyes popping, and he said, 'Don't you understand, I *did* kill the president. Kennedy would have been president. And if he was that pro-Israel when he wasn't president, imagine how he would be as president. So I decided to change history.' "

Sirhan says he never read the *Playboy* piece, but that he heard about it as it was passed around the prison, and that it is all libelous lies. "He concocted a pretty damn good story, and it was all phony," he says.

And he does not want to talk about the power of political assassins. He believes it is dangerous. He gets letters, sometimes, which he prefers not to discuss in detail — but they are letters that suggest others have watched him, and studied what he did, and thought about doing it themselves. He does not answer the letters. He tears them up. He says they disturb him.

He says he cannot entertain social and political what-ifs — not publicly, anyway. "I regard myself as being a disenfranchised person," he says. "I have no right to discuss that."

>*disenfranchise: to disenfranchise ... to dispossess of the rights of a citizen or of a privilege, as a voting, holding office, etc.*
>–*Webster's New Collegiate Dictionary. 1961*

'A VICTIM ALL HIS LIFE'

Mary Sirhan, voice quickening, the rs rolled softly in the Arabic way: "He was a victim all his life, since he was a baby and a child, and when he was growing up, till he was 13 years of age in Jerusalem, all he has seen, he never had a childhood, never was happy, never laughed, all he has seen is fear, hunger, dying, human beings in pieces, it's hard enough for a big man, but for a child — and we came here. And look what happened to him."

Sirhan Bishara Sirhan was born in Jerusalem, the son of a Christian Arab, employe of the public works department. Palestine had been under British mandate since 1920, when the World War I Allied forces divided up the Ottoman Empire; Sirhan's father, whose family came from a village near Jerusalem called Taibeh, worked with apparent pride for the British Mandatory Government. The family was Greek Orthodox, and lived just outside Musrara, a middle-class mixed Arab and Jewish quarter, in a ground-floor apartment that looked onto a small yard with pine trees.

Sirhan was a baby in a city rumbling into civil war. Jewish immigration to Palestine had soared during the years of the Holocaust, despite the British government's 1939 declaration limiting the number of Jews who could legally enter the country, and by 1945 — a year after Sirhan was born — Palestinian Jews had been agitating violently for increased Jewish immigration quotas. The British handed the whole problem to the United Nations, which recommended that the nation be partitioned into separate Arab and Jewish states.

The U.N. resolution passed in November 1947. The British withdrew from Palestine on May 14, 1948. In the intervening months, according to both his parents, the boy Sirhan watched the fury that was ripping Jerusalem in two, watched the bombing of Damascus Gate, where a crowd of Arabs had gathered to wait for the bus. Mary Sirhan, in an earlier interview, remembered her son saying, "Mamma, the bomb came down and made the people's blood run down there at Damascus Gate."

Mary Sirhan says he watched shooting, watched dynamite bombing, watched the death of his older brother, watched the disembowelment of a man, close up: "The bomb came and hit, and made a big ditch in the floor, and came up, and that man and his stomach and all the things in his stomach were brought out to the ground. And Sirhan was there, and many other children were there also, and they came running to me, and they said, 'Sirhan is lying on the ground'.... He wasn't hurt, but he was fainting because of fear."

GOOD REPORT CARD

In May 1948, according to Sirhan's mother, the family left the Musrara apartment during a predawn lull in the fighting over the newly divided Jerusalem. They fled — leaving their belongings behind, Mary Sirhan says — to an Arab-sector house which, according to testimony at Sirhan's trial, was shared with nine other families. Sirhan went to the Lutheran school. He was quiet, absorbed by the Bible (which he is said to have studied every evening) and deeply anti-Zionist. "Arabic, very good," reads his 1955-1956 school report. "English, good; Geometry, good ... Natural History, satisfactory ... Conduct, good; Diligence, good."

Sirhan's father had lost his job. He was by all reports a proud man so rigid in his religious and disciplinary beliefs that it is said — although he has denied it — that he sometimes beat his children. "Because of the frustration, you know," Mary Sirhan says. She says they struggled for the next eight years, eating rationed food and parceling out what money her husband had been able to save. In 1956, sponsored by a Pasadena family Sirhan's father had met in Jerusalem, the Sirhans emigrated to the United States under a special program for Palestinian refugees.

They came by boat to New York. Sirhan was fascinated by vending machines. He would examine the back of the machines, trying to figure out where the coffee and chocolate bars came from. "Mamma," Mary Sirhan says he asked her, "if we are Americans, are we going to be blond very soon?" His sister kept flushing the toilet, crying, "God bless America!" And all the way to Pasadena, on the crowded train that carried the family across the country, Sirhan looked out the windows into the rocking January snows — watching, his mother says now, for something that looked like the stone houses of Jerusalem.

In 1956 Robert F. Kennedy, 31-year-old counsel to the Senate Permanent Subcommittee on Investigations, had spent the autumn with the presidential campaign of Adlai Stevenson. When Stevenson lost, Kennedy returned to his Senate work and directed his attention to racketeering in the American labor movement.

An ally, in the investigation told Kennedy, "Unless you are prepared to go all the way, don't start it."

Robert F. Kennedy replied, "We're going all the way."

AUGUST 21, 1979

Second of two parts

He wants children. He thinks he would like them to go to church.

"I see many of these children, in this room ... when the families of these children come in, with all the little toddlers," Sirhan Bishara Sirhan says. He looks around quickly at the hospital-green walls of Soledad prison, the bathroom with its door left ajar, the small barred window and the August sun outside. "And I often wonder when I'm going to have my issue."

Issue: Robert Kennedy's assassin, taut and compact in his California prison dungarees, sits in the maximum security conference room and speaks of family with an odd, faintly biblical formality.

"Just a few days ago, I was rereading the Magna Carta, and the history that led up to it," he says, as though the thought has just struck him. "Those members of the parole board seem to me to be a true reincarnation of King John himself."

His pronunciation is careful, still softened by the spare traces of an Arabic accent. He sprints through references to the Constitution: "My due process... my equal protection rights... the Sixth and Fourteenth Amendments." Does he know the Preamble?

Sirhan Sirhan squints, considering, and smiles. "We, the people..." he stops, sits back in his chair.

"I'm too nervous," he says.

The room goes quiet.

Sirhan shakes his head.

"Hold these truths to be... self... it'll come to me... self-evident, and all that." He looks distressed. "Wasn't it Jefferson's authorship?"

He wanted once, to be a jockey. It was 1963, five years before he walked into the Ambassador Hotel and fired a loaded gun at Robert Kennedy's head. Sirhan was a teenager, a bookish Palestinian immigrant in Pasadena, Calif. "He wants to do something, to live, to be happy," says his mother, remembering, "And when he tried and was accepted, he used to take care of the horses. And he wanted to learn a lot about them."

Sirhan graduated from high school at 19. He was older, smaller, and darker-skinned than many of his classmates, who would dredge up memories afterward for the reporters who came scrambling: "So weak and scrawny, but always so neat... won a prize as one of the best in the candy sale... a very hard worker after school... calm and well-mannered... withdrawn, alone."

He had worked hard at his English, which was so unfamiliar to him when he arrived in Pasadena that other schoolchildren, according to the Sirhan biography by Godfrey Jansen, used to toss obscenities at him so he would repeat them later without knowing what they meant.

His father had left the family, returning to Taibeh after what Mary Sirhan says was a dismal seven months in southern California; she remembers her husband trying to beat Sirhan with a garden hose because the boy had stepped in some wet cement. "He wasn't respected, as he used to be in the old country," she says. "That was very hard on him. He used to be nervous, very nervous." Hesitant with his English, and unfamiliar with the American versions of the machines he had once used, Sirhan's father had not been able to hold a job, Mary Sirhan says. When he left, he took what money the family had.

Sirhan spent a year and a half at Pasadena City College but dropped out, his mother says, in part because he was distressed by his sister's death from leukemia. He took a series of jobs working in service stations and as a gardening assistant, and then got hired on at the Santa Anita racetrack. He cleaned stables. He exercised horses, and walked them to cool them off. He wanted to ride the way a jockey rides, but the scrawny, neat boy from John Muir High was 5 feet 4 and 120 to 125 pounds, and that, for a jockey, was just too big.

On September 25, 1966, in a southern California fog at the racetrack near the town of Corona, Sirhan was thrown from a filly he was exercising and was knocked unconscious. He was taken to a nearby hospital with a bloody face, and although he was released without report of serious injury, he quit riding a few months later and spent much of the next year complaining of blurred vision and pain in his eyes. He filed a workmen's compensation claim — settled finally for $2,000 — and for much of the following year, his mother says, Sirhan was edgy, unemployed, and discouraged about job prospects.

"He wants to be alone to read," Mary Sirhan says. "No lawyer wants to take his case, and that makes him more nervous. He says, 'Why? Is it because I don't have cash or what?' If he stops reading, you know, he looks at himself like this . . . like he has to stay, and get well, and nobody could help with his medical insurance . . . "

He took a job at the Pasadena organic food store. It was a small place, stocked with raw milk, fertile eggs and vitamin jars, and the owner, a vegetarian Seventh-day Adventist named John Weidner, used to talk to Sirhan about religion and the state of the world. Weidner had run a Dutch underground resistance organization during World War II, set up to rescue refugees from the Nazis, and he and Sirhan often sparred philosophically over American society and the future of the Middle East.

"He hated the Jews," Weidner says. "He would say that they had taken his home, his belongings, away, and that now they wanted to govern him [in Jerusalem] and he had no freedom there.... He thought that in America there was no chance for the little guy. Basically I think it was because he believed he was a great man, and he was an underdog."

Sirhan claimed to have seen an Israeli soldier cutting an Arab woman's breast, Weidner says. Weidner took him to a movie about Arab-Jewish relations in Israel, one that ended on a relatively tranquil note, and Sirhan announced afterward that the film was "baloney." He resented taking orders. He was a steady and reliable worker, Weidner says, but his pride was wounded so easily that in March 1968, when Weidner asked Sirhan why he had reversed some delivery directions, Sirhan flared up, said Weidner was calling him a liar, and ended up by quitting his job.

"He had no friends," Weidner says. "he was a lonely guy, always alone. Always alone.... If I may say what my opinion is, this guy had a terrific pride, like many people did. They think many things about themselves. And he was not recognized. People do all kinds of crazy things to be recognized. So I think that it was boiling in, boiling in, boiling in, I have to do something. And then I think he started to think about killing. I think he had planned to kill someone, or something, to have a big name."

Sirhan Sirhan was 24 years old and unemployed again. he had begun to study the occult sciences, and Rosicrucian mysticism. "He would tell me there are bodies in the universe that we see out of the corners of our eyes, but never bring into focus, and he was trying to focus on them," testified a family friend at his trial. He had read about "cyclomancy," which he described in his own testimony as "nothing but white magic ... you can take a pan of hot boiling water and put your hands in it and think cool and it was cool . . . and I did it the other way around, I took ice water and put my hand in it and thought hot and it was hot."

In 1968 Robert F. Kennedy announced he was campaigning for the Democratic presidential nomination.

He appeared in May in a television documentary, which was aired in the Los Angeles area and included a reference to the senator's visit to Israel in 1948, when as a young Harvard graduate he wrote a series of dispatches on the Arab-Israeli war for the *Boston Post.* Sirhan Sirhan was home at the time, watching the program.

"He was laying in the living room, in front of the television," Mary Sirhan says. "He even beat the television with his foot. I said, 'Why did you do that?' He said, 'People don't know what they're doing.'"

"They showed on the television where Robert Kennedy was in Israel helping to, so I thought, helping to celebrate the Israelis, sir, there, and the establishment of the state of Israel," Sirhan testified. "And the way that he spoke, well, it just bugged me, sir. It burned me up. And up until that time I had loved Robert Kennedy. I cared for him very much, and I hoped that he would win the presidency until that moment, sir . . . but he was doing a lot of things behind my back that I didn't know about. . . . At that time the way I felt about it, if he were in front of me, so help me God, he would have died."

"Kennedy must be assassinated," Sirhan wrote in his notebook, "before June 5."

Kennedy declared publicly, on several occasions, that the United States owed military aid to Israel.

"Sirhan Sirhan must begin to work on upholding solving the problems and difficulties of assassinating the 36th President of the United States," Sirhan wrote in his notebook.

He was going to target practice with a secondhand Iver Johnson pistol borrowed from one of his brothers, and reportedly appeared six times at gun ranges before June 4.

A columnist in the *Pasadena Independent Star-News* chastised Kennedy for simultaneously advocating American military aid to Israel and military withdrawal from Vietnam. News reports after the assassination said that column — along with a car key, four hundred-dollar bills, a five-dollar bill, four singles, and change — was found in the pocket of the "swarthy-skinned assailant," as UPI's photo caption called him, who fired at Kennedy's head in the Ambassador Hotel.

"As far as the loss of a human being, loved by his family and all that; loved by his children — on that basis, my action was totally undefensible," Sirhan says. "I acknowledge that. And I'm willing to pay the price. But as far as a politician, a self-seeker, getting votes and preferring one ethnic group against another in this great democracy, for personal interest, I have no — what's the word? I don't feel that he was ever fair in that respect."

Sirhan prefers to avoid talk of the past: "The slate has been sort of wiped clean," he says. "A new tabula rasa."

His parole date, which was just moved up by four months, has now been set at November 1984. The nation of Libya has offered him asylum, Sirhan says, but he does not want to spend five more years reading Arabic magazines in PHU 1.

He wants out.

"As far as murders go — I know how heinous and callous it might sound on my part to speak of it like that — as far as murders go, Robert Kennedy's death was not, ma'am, first degree murder," he says. "And it does not warrant, as far as my opinion goes, the imposition of first degree murder as the California law allows . . . in my case, the element of malice aforethought, which is a requisite for legal authorities to obtain, was missing."

What is an example of a true first degree murder?

"They had one guy in here one time who after he shot his victim decapitated him and fornicated with his head," Sirhan says heatedly. "That is first degree murder. They have guys who kidnap children, and do the same thing with them. They had this doctor, he killed his wife over a lengthy period of time, and tortured her. Execution-style murders are first degree murders, or at least deserving the maximum punishment. I can't be held totally responsible for the act of firing bullets from that gun. After the first shot, I was not in control of that gun."

He pays attention to the news, and he followed the conviction of former San Francisco supervisor Dan White, who shot to death Mayor George Moscone and supervisor Harvey Milk in what White's attorney described as a fit of rage. White was convicted of voluntary manslaughter. His prison sentence was seven years, eight months.

"Who was Robert Kennedy?" Sirhan demands. "Was he a greater creation of God? Was he more loved by God than, say, Moscone or Milk?

"Take Robert Kennedy, ma'am. Had he murdered a common citizen on the street, how would society have treated him? Would they have wanted him locked up for the rest of his life because he was a bad man? Chappaquiddick illustrates that. Dan White's trial illustrates that. What makes those lives any less valuable than Robert Kennedy's?"

Suppose one offers — as argument, not as legal theory — the suggestion that it does not matter how Sirhan committed the murder, or how he felt at the time. He assassinated a presidential candidate. He sabotaged the American political process. Is that perhaps so enormous a crime that he deserves to spend the rest of his life in prison?

"I offered the American people my life in the gas chamber," Sirhan says. (He is reported to have told the judge at his trial that he would rather plead guilty and face execution than allow people to believe he was receiving a fair trial.) "I never bargained with them to waste it and rot away in these prison dungeons, and do nothing but sit and collect resentment, which is what I've been doing these last few years. The whole thing is contrary to the theory of rehabilitation."

Sirhan smiles, expansive, touches his chest. "Do I seem degenerated or unrehabilitated to you?"

Where would he go?

"That call — that call back home still plays in my mind," he says. He means Palestine, but he says he would go anywhere in the Arab world. "They're all people of my heritage, and I relate to them all," he says.

"I was reading *Time* magazine a few months ago, where Rosalynn Carter was talking on the theme — everybody needs roots, where you can call home. And that hit me. That made me like those people. Where the hell is my homeland? Where are my roots?"

He has said he would fear for his safety even in the main prison area, and certainly on the public streets. Would he want to stay in American if he did not think it dangerous?

"I've been in this country over 22 years, and well over half of them I've spent in prison," Sirhan says. "After I've seen how the system works — you probably did read the book called *The Ugly American,* with all the machinations employed in that. I would still say that ugliness exists, ma'am. I want no part of it, to be honest about it . . . that Statue of Liberty means nothing to me. I hate to say that. But to be frank and honest about it, it means nothing to me. In fact, it means the opposite of what it says, because I have been victimized by this country, deprived of my homeland, dispossessed."

On June 6, 1978, the widow and brother and children of Robert Francis Kennedy drove to Arlington National Cemetery for a memorial service to mark the

10th anniversary of his murder. The service was held in the early evening, on the portico of the Custis-Lee Mansion in plain sight of the eternal flame over President John F. Kennedy's grave. A thousand people stood on the open grass nearby, listening. Michael Kennedy, who was 10 the night his father died, read from a speech Robert Kennedy had made in Cape Town, South Africa.

"... Let us then give our strength and our sweat, our lives and our labor, and together we will make a hemisphere full of such freedom's sons as will make the earth sing and tremble in their passing," Michael Kennedy read.

His mother walked to the grave, stood for a while in the settling darkness, and then gathered her children and drove away.

SEPTEMBER 7, 1979

This is what Joyce Bichler remembers:

"By January of '72, I couldn't deny it anymore, because the bleeding had really been quite heavy. There was one time when I would stand up, and it felt literally like I was hemorrhaging, and I couldn't get to the bathroom in time... I remember sitting in the doctor's office with my mother and sister... I remember asking him, 'What are the chances of its being cancer?' And I remember how defensive he got. He said, 'Don't even use that word'...

"And when they said, 'vaginectomy,' I just, you know, I really felt everything spin.

"Because I had never heard of such a thing before. I didn't know how they could do it."

Vaginectomy: the surgical removal of the vagina. The surgeons also removed Bichler's uterus, Fallopian tubes, appendix and left ovary. She was 18 years old.

This is what Anne Needham remembers:

"When (the doctor) did do the internal exam, he just freaked. He jumped up and said,

'Oh, my God, I've never seen anything like this before.' I went into shock. He ran across the room ... he called the nurse in. He said to her, 'Look at this'. He said, 'You've got to go to the hospital. You've got to go to the hospital right now.'"

One of Needham's vaginal tumors was the size of a dime; the second was the size of a nickel. Her vagina, along with the rest of her reproductive system, was surgically removed. She was given an artificial vagina, made from the grafted tissue of her buttocks. She was 20 years old.

On April 22, 1971, in a startling article in the *New England Journal of Medicine,* a Boston physician named Arthur Herbst reported that during the previous five years, he had examined eight young women with an extremely rare form of vaginal cancer. The disease was called clear-cell adenocarcinoma. It was deadly if not rapidly treated, and its sudden appearance in girls as young as 15 was so extraordinary that Herbst and his colleagues at Massachusetts General Hospital had pored through the patients' records, trying to find some medical link.

They found it. During pregnancy, the mothers of seven of the young women had taken a widely prescribed synthetic estrogen called Diethylstilbestrol, or DES. From 1941 on, despite published reports linking estrogens with cancer in laboratory animals, the drug had been given to hundreds of thousands of women (the figures vary, but estimates range up to two million) as a way to prevent miscarriages or bleeding during pregnancy. The Herbst study, and those that followed it, established that daughters born to these mothers were likely to have a condition called adenosis — the presence of mucous-producing nonmalignant tissue in the vagina — which required frequent and costly medical exams.

And in some cases — .14 to 1.4 per thousand, according to a Herbst follow-up — DES daughters developed clear-cell adenocarcinoma.

Vaginectomy was the most widely accepted treatment, for those who lived.

Joyce Bichler's mother had experienced bleeding.

Anne Needham's mother had suffered two miscarriages.

Six weeks ago in the New York State Supreme Court in the Bronx, a six-person jury ruled that Eli Lilly & Co., one of the largest early producers of drugs containing DES, must pay $500,000 in damages to Joyce Bichler. Even though Bichler could not prove that Eli Lilly made the specific DES product that her mother took, the jury accepted the argument of Bichler's attorney: that Lilly was one of the largest early manufacturers of DES, that DES was inadequately tested before marketing, that DES caused Bichler's cancer, and that Lilly must therefore assume the responsibility.

Two weeks ago, in a second suit in Chicago, a jury awarded $800,000 damages to Anne Needham. Needham's mother, unlike Bichler's, had found clear records of the precise drugs she had taken — her husband was the pharmacist who filled the prescription. White Laboratories, the New Jersey-based company that manufactured the drug, was found to have been negligent in its testing and marketing of DES. As Needham's attorneys argued in closing, the drug "scarred her, physically as well as emotionally, for life."

The Michigan attorneys who argued Needham's case have lawsuits pending on behalf of about 315 DES daughters in 18 states. In Boston, a U.S. District judge has agreed to hear what may develop into a multimillion-dollar class action against six drug companies on behalf of Massachusetts DES daughters.

One New York law firm has lawsuits demanding $20 million in punitive damages on behalf of each of three DES daughters — one of whom has since died of cancer. There are suits pending in almost every state in the nation, and the sums of money involved are potentially large enought to dwarf the estimated $141 million paid out to young victims of the West German-made sedative called Thalidomide.

White Laboratories is witholding comment on the Needham case, while the company decides whether to appeal. Eli Lilly has already filed an appeal. "If we're responsible for whatever a drug company does, whether it was our drug or not, you've changed the whole tort system in the United States," says Edwin Heafey, an Oakland attorney who has represented Lilly for 22 years.

He says the predistribution testing was extensive, and conducted by the leading researchers of the day.

And it cannot be conclusively proven that DES causes vaginal or cervical cancer, Heafey says. "We're talking, in the cancer situation worldwide, about a very small, minute incidence of the disease," he says. "Twenty-five percent of the people that die in America this year will die from cancer. Then you take the 346 (the number of young women listed since 1971 in an international tabulation of clear-cell adenocarcinoma cases) and how many were exposed to estrogen/230. (So) Twenty-five percent (of them) had the same thing and were not exposed to DES ... There's something else going on in the girls that have it, and I really believe that."

THE CONSTANT REMINDER

"I was the underdog," Joyce Bichler says, "and they were the big guys, and going into that trial they were laughing at us. They didn't think we had a chance. And we just stuck in there and fought back. And we won."

Bichler is 25 now, a San Francisco social worker with wiry dark hair and blue-gray eyes that do not flinch as she talks about the raw details of her medical history. She is married to a speech pathologist, whom she loved seven years ago when she became ill in New York, and who would not go away after her operation, despite Bichler's insistence that no man could ever find her attractive again.

"It's something that is brought to mind every single night of your life," Bichler says slowly. She is sitting on her living room couch, hands in her lap, absently twisting her gold wedding ring. "It's not like — I guess there are some surgeries where you just have a hysterectomy, you can forget about it and kind of go on living. But with this type of surgery you have the outward appearance of being okay . . . but in your private life, you can never really forget what happened."

Slower still.

"It's something you have to face constantly."

In 1971 she was a freshman, hesitantly premed, at State University of New York at Stony Brook. When she first noticed that her menstrual periods seemed longer and more frequent, she blamed the change in habitat — she had never lived away from home before. But by early 1972, when the blood was coming between periods and she sometimes thought she would faint, Bichler went to a doctor.

"The first thing he asked my mother was, did you take anything during pregnancy with me?" Bichler says. "And my mother said yes, she remembered specifically taking something, but she couldn't remember what it was."

Bichler's mother, in her two previous (and successful) pregnancies, had bled during the first three months of each. The new doctor monitoring the pregnancy with Joyce urged Mrs. Bichler to take DES.

There was nothing particularly unusual about the doctor's advice. Thirteen years earlier, a husband-and-wife doctor team at Harvard University had begun a series of tests on pregnant women which led them to conclude that DES helped prevent miscarriages and generally improve pregnancy. By the 1960s, some researchers had come to believe that DES does not prevent miscarriages after all — but in 1954, when Bichler was born, the conclusions of the Harvard team were still accepted by many doctors.

But there was also a body of medical opinion — some of the studies go back as early as the 1930s — which linked estrogens to cancer in laboratory animals. Why hold the drug companies responsible for not heeding these studies, while exempting the doctors? David Fine, the Cambridge attorney working on the Massachusetts class action suit, says drug companies are expected to be the final authorities on all medical research concerning their products. "It's just impractical to expect that a single physician would keep current with active literature affecting all the drugs he prescribes," he says.

Joyce Bichler was in the hospital for a month. She remembers waking to the sound of her own screams, seeing the blurred faces of her mother and boyfriend in the room, and slipping back under the painkillers. The surgeons left in one ovary and a small portion of her vagina, which they told her she would be able to stretch enough for an altered but functional sex life. Then Joyce Bichler left the hospital, went home to the Bronx, and shut herself up in her bedroom.

She snapped at her boyfriend, picking fights, convinced he must really want to leave her: "I couldn't understand how any guy could still like me," she says. "I really thought. 'This is it. No man is ever going to look at me.'"

Six months after the operation, as the family sat around the dinner table one night, they began to talk about a lawsuit.

There were two possible obstacles that have continued to hamper other DES suits over the years. First, statutes of limitation: In Illinois, for example, a DES daughter must sue within two years after she learns the drug made her ill. And in some states, such as New York, the countdown begins not with discovery of the injury but with the injury itself — so that if a woman learns she has cancer after the statute of limitations has expired, she may be without legal recourse.

Because of New York state law, Bichler was safe there. But like thousands of other DES daughters, she was never able to find the precise record of the drug her mother took. Many of these dated medical files have been lost over the years; organizers in DES task forces say they have heard so many stories of records that were burned up in office fires that they suspect a few physicians are deliberately lying or destroying files to avoid lawsuits.

Bichler's attorneys, led by former New York State Supreme Court Justice Leonard I. Finz, decided on an unusual approach. They would select a major, early producer of DES — Eli Lilly & Co. They would declare from the start that there was no way to prove Lilly made Mrs. Bichler's drug — but that the drug companies had shared a common responsibility to test DES more thoroughly before marketing the drug. It was a premise untested in the American courts, and it worked.

NOT EVEN A WORRY

"There was no drug, as of 1947, as investigated as estrogen," Heafey, the Lilly lawyer, says. He sits at the desk in his ninth floor law office, flanked by bound transcripts from the Bichler and Needham trials, shaking his head. "Put yourself back in 1941 and '47, and try to figure out what kind of airplanes we were flying, what kind of technology it was. .... There was no one that even suggested, in writing, a worry, just a worry, that there'd be a side effect on the offspring."

Did Lilly test the effectiveness and carcinogenic potential of DES before marketing it?

"Lilly relied on the universities to do all the testing," Heafey says, "Harvard, the best people. ... If I were Lilly, and you gave me $100 million, and you said, 'Okay, go test the drug in 1947, the best persons to have test that drug were White (Dr. Priscilla White, a respected Boston physician and researcher) and the Smiths (Drs. George and Olive Smith, the doctors who originally promoted the use of DES for spotting and miscarriages): They were the state of the art. They knew more about this subject than anybody alive."

Furthermore, Heafey says. Lilly did run animal tests on DES — at least six, according to the company's now-incomplete files. He denies the charge by Bichler's attorneys that those tests were inadequate to ferret out carcinogenic potential.

What about the medical research that linked estrogens to cancer in laboratory animals?

Heafey spreads his palms. "The other day they gave a mouse peanut butter and he got cancer," he says. "If that knowledge really meant what the rhetoric of the plaintiffs' lawyers say it means, why are they still using estrogens?

"... That's the trouble with animal studies," Heafey says. "They're informative, but you can't go crazy when you read them.... There are a lot of things that are carcinogenic in animals that are not in humans. The doctors knew that, and they know it now."

Members of the national task force called DES Action have said from time to time that if drug companies had contributed more time or money to the afflicted women, the companies might not be facing such massive legal problems today. Reaction?

"Lilly has spent, since 1971, in excess of a million dollars for assistance and grants and support of DES clinics and symposiums and a colloquium in New Orleans," Heafey says. "They sent out 240,000 letters to medical doctors . . . notifying them of the first Herbst report."

He says that in 1976 alone, Lilly gave $210,000 to research grants for the study of DES and its complications, and that much of the research in the first five years after the Herbst report was directed toward finding out "whether the adenosis girl was in trouble."

Although adenosis — the vaginal condition which shows up in many DES daughters — is not in itself harmful, the condition was thought at first to be precancerous; a few women with adenosis, in what is now considered extreme overreaction, were given vaginectomies. There is still no consensus as to whether the condition has much chance of changing to cancer, but some DES daughters with extensive tissue changes must undergo semi-annual exams that cost $100 or more with a special instrument called a colposcope.

Heafey says Lilly has not funded such exams. As to whether the adenosis girl was in trouble, "the conclusion," he says, "was that she is not."

Heafey finds it appalling that his company must share the blame simply because it produced and distributed DES.

"I think it's all over for pharmaceutical companies or for drug research if that ever became the law," he says. "The ball game is over. It's all in the brief. Talk about *money*. People forget that drug companies are made up largely of doctors. They're not made up of some Wall Street, pin-striped — I go back to Lilly and they're all wearing smocks. I go back in their labs, and they're all breaking their tails trying to figure out what causes cancer."

One more thing. "This drug wasn't a money-maker, either," Heafey says. "Christ. It was a very, very small shelf item for Lilly."

STARK TERROR

In 1973, when Anne Needham was a 20-year-old junior college student in Chicago, she developed a rash under both arms. She changed deodorants. The rash eased and then got worse. Her dermatologist suggested she see a gynecologist, noting that a yeast infection sometimes causes rashes. Needham made the gynecologist appointment and went shopping for a birthday card with her boyfriend.

She was standing in the store, she says, when she felt stabbing pains in her abdomen. She started to bleed. She thought she had better sit down fast, and as she was heading out of the store toward their parked car, Anne Needham blacked out.

The doctor who treated her — who found the tumors, who ordered the biopsy, who called Mrs. Needham and labored over telling her what would have to happen — had delivered the baby Anne. "He kept saying, 'Anne, we'll take care of it, don't worry about it,'" Anne Needham says. "I was thinking, my God, can they take this out of my body, has it spread, has it metastasized.... It wasn't until afterward that I got to the clinic and realized what they were going to do."

Carefully, voice in check, Mary Needham says into the telephone from Chicago: "It was a long time before I realized that the responsibility in a sense was mine, because I did not want to abort this baby. I had lost two babies previously before I became pregnant with Anne. She has always been a treasure, as all children are . . .

"They kept hounding me with this idea that I had taken this drug that had caused cancer in the fetus." Mrs. Needham says. Her voice is breaking.

"You go through such hell. . . . First of all you go through a horrible terror, a stark terror. The first girl (at the hospital with the same condition as Anne's) had passed away. . . . You see your daughter crawl on the floor because she can't stand up, can't talk and can't walk. . . . Yes. You do feel guilty. Stark terror. You don't know whether she's going to live or die."

Anne Needham's vaginectomy and hysterectomy were conducted at the Mayo Clinic in Rochester, Minn., one of four government-aided DES centers in the country. She remembers how the moments of clarity pinged odd and improbable in the hours before her reproductive system was cut away: would it work, would she live, would the skin graft from her buttocks make a scar above the bikini line and please could the doctors be careful about that because she had already picked out her new swimsuit.

Needham came home in late March 1974 — cramping, hobbled, and slightly incontinent. "You feel like a little old lady," she says. "It didn't start to hit me, I don't think, until about six months later . . . I really blocked a lot of it out of my mind . . . I felt like I had this word *cancer*, imprinted on my face. . . . I felt like it made me older, real fast."

It was not until the Mayo Clinic sent routine questions to the Needham family, asking whether Mrs. Needham had taken any hormones during her pregnancy that the family looked back into the records and discovered that Anne Needham was a DES baby. The drug was called Dienestrol. "I didn't really realize what I was getting into." Anne Needham says. But she sought out legal help.

She thinks, now, that she may go back to school. Once she wanted to be a nurse, but now she does not know what she wants. She has broken up with her boyfriend. She can bicycle, and jump rope and walk without pain. "I still have a lot more growing up to do," Anne Needham says.

Joyce Bichler thinks she and her husband will adopt children. "It's a real blow to know you don't have the choice," she says.

And the money?

"Nothing can pay for what happened," Bichler says. "There's really no amount that can compensate.... But the real victory is in the verdict. We have put the drug companies on notice, saying that all drugs they put out must be safe and effective — and that they must be held accountable."

She says this near the beginning of the interview, in what sounds like the voice of a public figure: quiet, strong, assured. The edge comes later.

"It's just — " Bichler hesitates. "it's not something that just happened. I've got cancer, and at least I'm alive. But it's the feeling that *it never should have happened*. It could have been prevented. It should have been prevented. But it never should have happened to me. And that is very difficult to live with."

CONVERSATIONS

CLARK: It must be an interesting job to be writing for the Style section of "The Washington Post" out of the San Francisco area.

GORNEY: My basic problem is that I don't feel that I belong in newspapers. This is the only newspaper job in the country that I could do well at. I can write a story on deadline, but I don't particularly like doing it. Basically, I love doing research. The single thing that I'm proudest of is the Sirhan story which I spent a long time on. The constant tension in my work in newspapers, and this is not a complaint, is that I always want to spend more time on a story. I want to become an expert in everything. I assume that ultimately I will write books. And in the interim that I will write for magazines.

What makes you uneasy about writing for newspapers?

A good example is a story I did when gold prices were going crazy. I had been mentioning that I wanted to go up into the gold country and do a story about the modern day gold boom. And all of a sudden the prices went crazy and my editor said "Go. Now. Instantly. We need this story." I went up to a mining town where the head of the Western Mining Council lives, spent one day learning the stuff you can learn in a day. There are some delicious complex environmental issues up there having to do with conflicts over the 1872 mining law. And I couldn't do them. I didn't have the time. I was so frustrated. I wasn't angry at my editors. I talked to them about it. They said, "We understand, but we have to have a gold story for Tuesday's paper." So I wrote it. And I was very unhappy. And I thought: Well, I don't think in the long run I belong doing this.

Are you saying that a good writer can't work for a newspaper?

I don't think that's true. Some of the best writing around is deadline writing. Some of the most vivid writing that I've ever seen is the stuff that foreign correspondents do. But it's hard and it requires real sensitive editors. No writer can work without a good editor. And I don't think a great writer can work without a great editor. First of all, great editors are few and far between. And an editor who really knows how to handle writing is not so likely to find a good and satisfying job on a newspaper because the constraints are so different. Most don't have time to do the kind of thing that Shelby Coffey (editor of Style section) manages to make time to do, which is to say: This passage doesn't quite work. Let's see if we can make it work.

Elaborate on what makes him a great editor.

I know there's a whole school of thought in newspapers that experienced, professional reporters just do it and don't need their hands held. I think that's crap. What makes an editor great is support. I don't know a writer who isn't insecure. An editor has to say: We think you're wonderful, we know you can do wonderful work. Even when your work is terrible. Second, there's some gift, a sensitivity to nuances in writing. There are some editors who can just read your copy and instinctively feel what's going to make it better and what is not.

If your story needs a lot of work, how does an editor provide negative criticism?

I'm fairly resilient about that sort of thing. Usually I know that a story is flawed. I just send it in anyway, because I'm confident that they're going to help me figure out what's wrong with it. A great editor will make you feel like a real trouper, a truly talented person for being able to fix a story, for being able to send something in that's flawed and then make it better.

Why don't you take us step by step through the process of writing the Sirhan story.

I wish I could tell you that I had done something really clever or fancy to get that interview. What I did was to call the prison and say, "Does he want to give an interview?" and the guy said, "Yeah." And I said, "What!" There was a brief news item that said Sirhan had been denied parole and I figured maybe he'd want to talk about it. He hadn't talked to anyone in 10 years except one thing with Dan Rather. So it was like this big scoop.

So the first thing I had to do was to find out everything I could. I was more nervous about this interview than I have ever been. I knew I would have a limited amount of time. I knew I wouldn't be able to do my standby—I always do a followup, even if it's just five minutes on the phone. I knew I wasn't going to be able to do a followup with Sirhan. I had this notion, which was silly, that somehow there was some single question which was going to open him up and be articulate about himself. As it happens he's enormously articulate about himself.

I did my normal procedure for preparing for an interview. I went back to the *Reader's Guide* in the public library and I read everything I could find about the assassination. There were several books that were written about him. There was one biography by an East Indian man, who took a Third World perspective, in no way condoning the assassination, but talking about Sirhan's Palestinian background. There were several books about the trial itself, and then there were all the assassination books.

Normally, in a big interview I'd spend a couple of days talking to people who knew the person I'm going to interview. That wasn't available in the case of Sirhan because he had changed lawyers a number of times. His current attorney is a criminal lawyer who doesn't know him well.

Then I just spent several hours thinking about the assassination and about Sirhan and wrote down questions. (A week had passed.)

We drove down there. They didn't give me a specific time limit, so I had no idea how much time I'd get to talk with him. It turned out to be about two hours. I brought two tape recorders, I was so nervous about one falling apart. The prison official said it was OK for me to use them. Sirhan didn't want it used. I explained that it would make the interview more accurate. But he said "No, no, I saw what they did to Nixon and his tapes." He was very worried that I would doctor the tapes in some way. So I took notes. I wrote like a fiend.

He also told me he didn't want any photographs taken because he was a hate object and was afraid that if Americans saw his photograph, it would enflame them against him. So I took a very big gamble. I brought a photographer anyhow and had him wait outside. Sirhan and I talked about a half hour, and I explained that his wish would prevail. And then I gave him the best sales job. I said, Look, we have to have a picture because this is a big story. If we don't have a picture of you now, the only ones available are the ones from the shooting. And you're going to look like a disheveled assassin with blood on his hands. And that is going to enflame people more than the way you look now. He's handsome in a Middle Eastern sort of way. And finally he said OK bring the photographer in and he got the most extraordinary pictures.

So when the interview was over we drove back. We drove about two hours in silence because I was filling out my notes. Somebody told me years ago: Whenever you come out of an interview, go back instantly and review your notes because you're not going to be able to read a quarter of what you wrote.

I read my notes over and over, and I usually circle quotes in three different colors, marking the quotes I know I'm going to use and the quotes that I think are good. By the time I've read them that many times, I know what's there. And I know the background material pretty well.

The way I start writing is always the same. I sit down at my typewriter and start typing. I start to babble, sometimes starting in the middle of the story, and usually fairly quickly I see how it's going to start. It just starts shaping itself on the typewriter. It was quite clear how the Sirhan story would begin. I liked the lead right away. I made it clear that this was his first interview in ten years with a newspaper, dropped in some of his strongest quotes: He thinks he's done his time now, he wants to go home. You have this interview. You have this historical event. You have your description of the person. You've got to set him up. You've got to place him in the context of history. You've got to tell the people what he said. And get his life story in there. So it wasn't hard to organize.

Do you rewrite a lot?

I rewrite paragraphs over and over. There is one paragraph in that Sirhan story that I rewrote more than any other paragraph I've ever rewritten: About whether he connects his act to the historical events that followed it. Whether he understands that he entirely changed the shape of the American 1970s. That was hard to say. I talked it out, wrote it out, and wrote it over and over. I crumpled up pages and threw them away. It was a process of just paring down and paring down and just trying to make it as clear and as short and as strong as I could.

Don't the quotations at the beginning and the end of the story—the ones about Kennedy and his family—charge the atmosphere against Sirhan?

I don't believe in hatchet jobs. I don't believe in making up a reader's mind. But, indeed, the quotes charge the atmosphere against him. But it was terribly important—to make it clear what he did. It was Shelby's idea to call somebody to talk about what Kennedy would have been doing if he had lived.

In these stories you interview many different characters. Are there any particular interviewing techniques that you rely on?

The essential one is to relax. And you have to be careful with notebooks and tape recorders. You don't use your notebook like a derringer. It makes people uneasy and that's understandable. So you go in and sit down and you just make conversation. So then they're relaxed. And then I bring the conversation around to the subject at hand and gently pull out the notebook.

I hate going into an interview without knowing a lot about the person. You put the person at ease and flatter them by making it clear that you've read about them, studied about them, so you find yourself for the first half hour asking these very informed questions. And then in the end you are in a position to ask the really naive questions which are always the ones that get you the best answers.

What about Joyce Bichler?

Joyce was a very easy person to talk to. We're the same age. We felt very simpatico right away. She is accustomed to her role as a spokesperson for DES daughters. She's incredibly composed. When you sit down in an interview like that you know that somewhere in the next hour you're going to be talking about her vaginectomy. And there was this moment (because I felt such sympathy) that the choice was for both of us to just sit there and cry or to go on with the interview. She has got to figure out for herself how much she wants to say. Do you want to tell some total stranger who's going to put it in the newspaper what your sex life is like? No. But also in the context of the story, you have to make it clear that it's had an effect on your sex life. So in this case I would say: Look, this is really sticky and you can answer any way you want to and you can refuse to answer but I have to ask you. Has it altered your sex life? She said Yes. But she clearly didn't want to talk about it any more and I didn't press her.

It requires genuine care. We go mucking around in people's tragedies. The hardest thing that any reporter faces is how not to go crazy with grief but at the same time respond the way a human being ought to respond. I cry a lot on stories. The first time it happened I thought, Now what kind of a reporter are you? You're supposed to be tough and aloof. That idea stayed with me for quite a while. If there is a reason that people are more inclined to talk to me about their private feelings, their tragedies, it's because I really feel it. And they can sense that. If you're sitting with some mother whose 15-year-old son drowned in a way that should not have happened, and she starts to cry, and you start to cry, you're not faking it, that's genuine pain.

To me it's important to give a little in an interview. Like at the Sante Fe prison riot. A lot of the cons who were killed in that riot were teenagers. I was talking to a woman whose brother had vanished in there. I have an 18-year-old brother, who I love dearly. I told her. We both just dissolved into tears. There was a bond there.

How about Dr. Seuss?

Well, Dr. Seuss was a little bit hard, but he was fun. He is sort of quiet about himself at first. But he's very intense and serious about his work. We were finally able to get some interesting talking done because I genuinely love Dr. Seuss.

I truly thought that *The 500 Hats of Bartholomew Cubbins* was one of the great books in America. I was thrilled to be doing the interview. I think he could see it. When I asked about specific characters, about the hats, he sort of lit up a bit. We talked at great length about Yertle the Turtle's relation to Nazi Germany. And he was tickled that I seemed to care about the process of creating the Lorax.

I liked that story a lot because the reporting is good. That sequence about trying to find the right color green for the parrot. I really liked that when Grace Clarke told me, because that's really how he is. A thoroughly methodical man. I learned that from talking to people at the art department. And his wife told me how he had this obsession with reading mystery books. If you can talk to a person's spouse that's real nice because they always know all these wonderful little details.

The frog story was different. There you're covering an event.

That was so much fun. I found a really good publicist for the frog jumping contest. He was funny and very sharp. He started giving me all this interesting detail. So I got the idea that I wanted to treat this one like *Sports Illustrated* at the Kentucky Derby. So we did it absolutely deadpan, but kept cracking up. There was a lot of beer up there. Everyone is either drunk or punchy through the entire weekend. So you go around and ask these people how they train their frogs and they just tell you. I had to get all the names of these things. Detail is very important in something like this. I'm a firm believer in lists. It was wonderful. I had a great time. I came back and just sat down and wrote that lead and started laughing.

I learned frogs. I've always joked that good reporters have the attention span of a very smart seven year old. For three days you just learn everything there is to learn. You keep asking questions over and over. Be absolutely straightforward about your ignorance. What is that? What does it mean? Explain it to me again.

How do you decide which details to use in a story?

The basic principle is: If it's interesting to me it's going to be interesting to most readers. When I read nonfiction prose that I love, the detail in it is usually profuse. Someone tells you that the particular kind of glass at the prison breaks into shards. It's creepy. It's scary. Shards make you shiver. I knew it had to go into the story.

Do you write down descriptive details in your notebook?

I have one trick I use in describing people. I ask the person a question that I really don't care about. And while the person is giving me the answer, I'm writing down what he looks like. People get nervous if they're not saying anything and you're writing stuff down.

You demonstrate great versatility in style in these stories. How do you develop that?

You have to read a lot. And when you find a writer you love, you read everything you can get your hands on by that writer. I've read compulsively since I was very young. Back in my brain somewhere there is serious nonfiction prose, funny prose. So you have to have an enormous variety of materials logged back there.

And this, I think, is the essence of feature writing. You have to be passionately interested in everything. You have to want to learn about frogs or cancer or assassins, everything there is to know. You have to know five times as much as you're ever going to use in the story. The only really essential quality of a writer is crazed curiosity.

Carol McCabe

1980 Prize Winner
News

COMMENTS

Skillful journalists are experimenting with a type of reporting that goes well beyond the traditional "human interest" story. Some are calling it "people journalism," but it should not be confused with the journalism of gossip and glamor, practiced more and more to attract readers to newspapers.

Reporters are centering their stories not only on the council meeting, the court decision or the administrative memo, but also on the people directly affected by public policy, the men and women and children who suffer from bad decisions regarding inflation, taxes or energy.

No one practices this type of journalism with more skill or dedication than Carol McCabe, as these five stories on the environment demonstrate. With instincts honed by 20 years as a reporter, McCabe has a knack for finding the people who will bring complicated stories to life for the reader.

She knocks on their doors, walks in their gardens, shares their meals, sleeps in their houses, becomes their friend. Her engaging personality and disarming demeanor—she can make herself look as inconspicuous as the second runner-up in a Pillsbury Bake-Off—put people at ease. They open up their minds to her, and their hearts.

The writing style reflects the reporter. It is graceful, direct, plain, not calling attention to itself, but letting interesting characters tell their own story.

Carol McCabe graduated with a degree in political science from Sweetbriar College. She worked six years at the *Washington Daily News* as a reporter, columnist and women's editor. After covering the 1960 presidential campaign, she served as a legislative assistant to two Congressmen.

She worked as a freelancer in Southeast Asia, including Vietnam, in 1961. Upon her return to America, she became the arts and humanities editor at the University of Rhode Island, where she still teaches courses in magazine and feature writing.

McCabe joined the *Providence Journal-Bulletin* in 1971 and in 1974 moved to the *Journal's* Washington Bureau. She returned to Providence and now specializes in news features for the Sunday paper.

She has won many writing awards, including the Ernie Pyle prize for the 1976 series on the Bicentennial.

Her lead to the story about structural damage to a nuclear plant in Connecticut typifies the style of these pieces. She creates a sense of place, introduces important characters and states the action in a dramatic form: "A gull's complaint hung in the air behind Nevio and Diana Petrini's house at Pleasure Beach on Thursday morning. November wind rustled bleached vanilla sea grasses and just offshore, a lobster boat working traps drew a circle in Niantic Bay. Then the moment was broken by an unsettling rumble from the Millstone nuclear complex, New England's largest power plant, directly across from Petrini's back yard. The sound had a primordial depth, like a tearing of the earth."

Traditionally, the endings of news stories contain their least important elements, and many news stories still peter out into insignificance.

McCabe works carefully on her endings. In the nuclear power story she leads the reader to a conclusion that symbolizes people's concerns about their future in a nuclear world: "On Thursday at Pleasure Beach, there were swans in the water and gulls in the air. Across the way, seven cranes hung above the construction site of

Millstone III. Behind the house...Nevio Petrini was mending his net. Next door, a new house is being built for a couple who will be able to move in just about the time their baby is born."

McCabe has a special gift as a reporter and interviewer, an ability to evoke strong statements from people. And, without condescension, she records them, catching the rhythms and regional flavor of their speech. For example, Maine farmer Blair Yeomans has this to say about the politics of a large insecticide spraying program: "That big green dollar is gonna kill this state...I don't know how they'd get such a product, but if they'd take this money for spray and buy some truth serum and spray it all over Augusta, it'd do more good, I think."

One possible weakness in her writing, her editor complains of it occasionally, is that she delays telling the news, letting the narrative carry the reader into the story. In her Wytopitlock story, for example, the news hook does not come until the 19th sentence: "The reason why Rita Potter and increasing numbers of other Maine residents have begun to fuss is that they wonder if the spray might not poison people as well as pests."

McCabe argues in favor of her approach in the interview which follows the stories. She is wonderfully articulate about her craft, and reflects upon her reporting, writing and interviewing techniques. She explains how she transforms a complex and potentially tedious subject, chemical pollution, into a compelling and fully-human drama.

MAY 27, 1979

WYTOPITLOCK, Maine — Thick clumps of old French lilacs are blooming beside the cellar holes and barren barns here, and the fields are moist and green. The barn swallows are back from Brazil, and if the ones up at Blair and Ruth Yeomans' house would stop their crazy swooping around, they might eat a few of the black flies. Meadow Brook and Little Meadow Brook are full of trout. The goose at Jim and Rita Potter's place, the one that lost its mate, is no longer in love with its own image reflected in the bumper of the pick-up since they gave it a mirror to adore.

Jim Potter takes off his boots outside the trailer after a day working in the woods. The boots are mud-crusty because the woods are full of runoff. The ridges are alive with water this time of year.

Potter, who was born on this place, has been in the woods for 30 years. He started out when he was seven or eight, working with his father, yarding logs with horses. Nowadays, he works with a skidder, cutting pulp for a contractor who sells his logs to a paper company.

Northern Maine is upholstered with eight million acres of spruce forest, growing crops of trees from which the mills will make toilet paper, paper towels, newsprint, and enough other products to account for about one-third of what economists call the "value-of-manufactures" in Maine. By comparison, the total value of all fish, raw forest products, potatoes and other agricultural products together account for only 16 percent of the total, and the tourist business to only about one-tenth.

"The truth of it is, the paper companies own this state, pure and simple," Jim Potter says as he pushes up the visor of his Johnson Chain Saw cap and goes inside. There, his wife, Rita, is working in her housecoat after bathing off the dust of the potato field where she works.

Rita, the mother of Victoria and Bret, is a beauty, with ash-blonde hair and eyes that light blue shade of full-skinned blueberries. Down at Augusta, she thinks, they probably call her that crazy broad in Wytopitlock. She's the one who has people all stirred up about the fact that again this year, as for the last decade, the paper companies, with the help of state and federal governments, will spray millions of acres, including sections in this area, with poisons designed to kill the spruce budworm. The budworm, a hungry larva that feasts on the new growth of spruce trees, must be sprayed, the state Department of Conservation says, or it will destroy $30 million dollars worth of spruce and fir this year alone.

Mrs. Potter got mad about the spraying last year and circulated a petition door-to-door in this end of vast Aroostook County to stop it.

The reason why Rita Potter and increasing numbers of other Maine residents have begun to fuss is that they wonder if the spray might not poison people as well as pests. Environmental activists are convinced that it might, and a federal environmental-impact statement, issued early this year, expressed some concern that health hazards might result from the pesticides. For the first time, the state this year admitted that the pesticide-spraying posed a health risk and ran advertisements urging that young children, pregnant women and breast-feeding mothers leave the spray areas.

"Spray Advisories" appear on letter-sized sheets tacked up in forest areas to be sprayed. "Conclusive scientific evidence is lacking that any of the spray materials being used in Maine this year are the cause of human disease when applied as proposed," the advisory reads, but the state suggests, "since effects on health remain under study, we recommend that persons who need not be in the spray areas and particularly those who may be especially susceptible to health risks, avoid the spray areas during the period of May 20 to June 20. . . . Persons who plan to be in the spray area and who are concerned about possible health hazards may wish to consult a physician for advice."

The advisory lists steps that campers, woodsworkers and others "who find themselves in an area being sprayed" should take, including changing clothes and washing skin with soap and water.

Gov. Joseph E. Brennan has defended the program, saying, "It's not a major, major risk," but concedes that the spraying is a trade-off between the need for wood fiber and the danger to public health. Rita Potter wryly says she thinks she'll send her son Bret, who's nine, down to stay at the governor's place until the danger period is over.

At the trailer alongside Route 171, Jim slides his lunch pail onto the kitchen counter. "What I base my argument on is this: They say there's no proof it is harmful. Well, by the same breath, they have to say there's no proof it isn't, don't they?"

"The state said last year that this would be a good place to test a new chemical because there were so few people here," Rita said. "Sometimes I think people hadn't protested before because they didn't realize for a long time that they were being polluted. Finally, last year, they began to see, and they signed my petition even though everybody around here works for the paper company — there's nothing else to work *for* — because, they'd say, 'My car got covered in oil and that must mean we're getting covered in oil,' or they'd say, 'My flowers all died.'"

"Budworm City," they call the project center at the airport in Millinocket, near Mount Katahdin and Baxter State Park. Here, officials from the Maine Forest Service direct the activities of about 100 persons involved in the $11-million program to spray an area of forest larger than Connecticut. Six million dollars will be paid to chemical companies for the four insecticides to be used: four million will pay for the aircraft and the pilots to fly them. A token $175,000 has been earmarked for environmental-monitoring projects to study effects on humans, brook trout, aquatic insects, and birds.

At an opening meeting of the pilots and chemical crews last Monday, Ernest Richardson, on loan to the budworm project from the Maine Division of Human Services, talked about the chemicals to be used and precautions to be taken. "Sevin (Carbaryl) has an excellent reputation. No one has ever complained of sickness, illness or any reaction, and that's something to brag about," he said of the insecticide that will be used most. Carbaryl has been under study by the Environmental Protection Agency since 1976, when it received evidence that the insecticide, which is sprayed over Maine forests in a kerosene solvent, causes birth defects in dogs.

"Orthene, well, in short, I'll tell you, it stinks terribly," Richardson told the spraying assembly. "It's pretty raunchy to work with, but pretty darn safe . . . Dialox is moderately toxic . . . Matacil is being used on an experimental basis, and it is the most toxic chemical we have the experience of using this year. We're gonna send this out on two very sound aircraft with very sound plumbing in 'em. The only thing that makes a guy shiver is having a plumbing failure in flight."

The pilots had been coming in from the south and west for nine days before the start of spraying last week, waiting for project director Ancyl Thurston to give the go-ahead and release the "blocks" of the map for spraying as the budworms reached the moment in their maturation when insecticides would be most effective.

At the motels in town, where the sauerkraut smell of the paper mill is a constant presence, suntanned men in cowboy hats and boots, Californians in sandals, bearded Vietnam vets and veterans of other wars paced the lobbies and fed the pay phones. The Alabaman was there, the pilot the others say is at least 60. He still eats, sleeps and dreams airplanes even though his war is history to most of the other guys. One of the planes of his war was there, along with a couple of Connies, a flock of C54s, PV2s, a couple of TBMs and helicopters, and five Thrush Commanders, the small crop-dusters that have been touted as useful in controlling spray drift. They've had some problems with that.

Last year, an elementary school was sprayed, and many individuals have reported spray drifting beyond buffer areas around settlements, highways, waterways, and the property of those who have asked not to be sprayed.

Mitch Lansky, who lives in Bancroft, raises bees. In 1976, he followed the procedures to request that his property not be sprayed, then went out and put markers at the tops of his tallest trees. "Within a week I got sprayed with Sevin," he recounts. "It was really early in the morning and I was going to work at a sawmill. I was standing right there when they flew directly over me. I could see the stuff descending around me and I was kind of crazy, standing there shaking my fist and shouting at them. There was white stuff and dead insects all over the place." Lansky received a $5,000 out-of-court settlement from the spraying contractor.

Efforts are made to prevent spray from drifting. Flights are made only in calm weather and at low speeds. The same precautions that make spraying safer for the people below, however, make it less safe for the pilots. No pilot has ever crashed during the Maine spraying program, but there have been close calls, particularly in a case last year in which two planes designed for antisubmarine warfare had to return to base fully loaded. The planes were not designed to land loaded. One observer reported seeing one PV2 bounce on the runway, then watching its pilot hit full throttle in an attempt to remain airborne, barely missing three aviation fuel trucks. According to that observer's report, the pilot landed on the next pass and later reported that he had nearly released all of the insecticide in the plane.

Program officials readily admit that the flights are hazardous. Project director Ancyl Thurston says that the pilots are well-paid. "They'd have to pay *me* well to fly 110-165 mph at treetop level."

"Lobotomy cases," one of the pilots at Budworm City calls his colleagues. Glenn Lemler of Flagstaff, Ariz., who runs a ski patrol in winter and sometimes works budworms in the spring as a navigator or guide-plane pilot, stood near the flight line in sandals and hiking shorts. "Those planes are graveyard relics that come alive in May. I don't mean they aren't in good mechanical shape. You can *bet* they're not going up until they're in good shape. But these guys are crazies. If they were to go down and the crash didn't get them, the juice (poison) would."

"There will be no dumping or spilling in any airport," Richardson told the pilots. "The storm drains (at the field in Mullinocket) drain toward a potential outlet for their drinking water. You will catch all spills in buckets and pails.... Let's make a steadfast decision that we're not going to spill." Tanks would have to be washed out between different chemicals, he said. "Nobody today wants responsibility for the dumping of toxic wastes. Most places ship the stuff to New Jersey, but someday even New Jersey won't want it. When it's time to flush your tank, fly your flushings somewhere out on the block (spray areas)."

The pilots were told how the chemicals work and what to do if they became contaminated. (Pilots are, obviously, exposed to a higher concentration of the toxin than anyone on the ground would be.) The chemicals, Richardson said, are essentially nerve poisons. "Overexposure inhibits the enzyme that allows the muscle to relax. That's how it kills the bug."

A contaminated pilot, he said, would first have some vision trouble. "That's the bad one — you lose your depth perception." Then, he said, there would be stomach cramps, partial paralysis of arms and legs, some breathing distress. Each flight crew, he said, would receive a bottle of atropine tablets as an antidote. "They are to be taken only if you feel you are becoming symptomatic. If you have a plumbing failure, pop one of these and come on home." Each crew, he said, would carry an agricultural respirator. "If you get doused, someone will take you back to your barracks or motel. Do not go alone. Change your clothes and wash by normal means."

Flying graveyard relics filled with nerve poison may be a high-risk job, but the pay is good. "Most of the pilots come away from this with seven or eight thousand dollars for about three weeks' work," Lemler, the navigation pilot, said. That's just about what Jim Potter the logger brings home from the woods in a year.

"The men in the woods have to go in, spraying or no spraying, or not get paid," Rita Potter said.

"Timber crews operating in the area may not have phones" (and therefore could not be notified that an area has been sprayed), a public-relations woman for the project said at Budworm City. "Of course most of them couldn't care less. They say, 'We've been sprayed before and we'll be sprayed again.' "

"One thing made me mad," Jim remembered. "There was one area we cut half of, one year. The next spring they sprayed it, and we went in to cut the next day. We cut everything. Somebody should have known all along we was going to cut there and there wasn't any point in spraying."

Jim Potter works with a machine called a skidder. "There's *no* way you can cut with a skidder and not knock down the young trees. They got one worse than that called a harvester that doesn't leave anything standing.

"They use softwood for pulp and they'd like to do away with the hardwood in these forests and have only softwood, farm it like a hayfield. They think they know more than nature did when it put hardwood there in the first place. The paper mills are increasing production every year, and they keep trying to think of how to grow more softwood.

"Well, if you start eating the chicken, you will be getting less eggs. They are lulling people into a false security by saying it's good for the economy to cut more wood and make more jobs. They're creating jobs, sure, but what's going to be left when they get done?" Potter is an amiable man with a Maine accent as thick as the woods around Blunder Pond. He says he has been radicalized by what has been done to the land around him.

"Any kind of radical there is up here, I guess I am now," he says.

Rita is English; they met when he was in Edinburgh in the Navy. "Her father, I guess he thought that Rita and I were goin' a bit on the radical side. He came to visit and he hadn't been here in five years. I said, 'Come in the woods and see.' He took a look around and he said, 'Bloody hell.' Just like that. 'Bloody hell, it looks like an A-bomb hit.'"

The barn swallows at Blair and Ruth Yeomans' house are swooping around, Blair says, because "we pulled down a barn pole this morning and they had to get out and find a new place. All the old barns is gone. The swallows have been down to Brazil all winter and they come back and go half crazy because there's no barns to nest in."

Blair is in his 70s and has lived on this place near the fire tower for 50 years, since he married Ruth. Ruth was born here, and so was her father. Blair is sitting this morning at the table that used to be full at haying time.

"It's an awful thing to see a town die. Once there was five farms up this road. It was the lack of market that killed them." Blair says. "All these farms was poor anaway. They had these farms up here to grow hay, horses to eat the hay, and boys to work the woods with the horses." When Blair says "horses," it has a special Maine sound: "husses."

"Well," he goes on, "it was in the first war that they started growing potatoes, and then pretty soon the market went and they were hauling potatoes out of here and dumping 'em. Then pretty soon the Federal Land Bank owned half the town of Drew."

Blair worked the woods. "Working the woods, we didn't make a third of what the men in the mills made. Every time they'd get a raise in the mills, the price in the woods would drop. They were unionized. There weren't any unions in the woods. They called us the last independent people and I guess we was. We paid for it.

"Now," Blair Yeomans says, "they're trying to build the woods over so it will be all stands of spruce and fir, no hardwoods. Cut everything down at once, and the first thing that comes back will be your balsam fir, which is what the budworm loves best of all. They're making what I'd call budworm heaven in the woods, and then they want to spray people with poison to kill the budworms. I told them that once on the television news, and they asked me what were my credentials. They wanted letters after my name. I said I got letters after my name: DDT."

"That book *Silent Spring* is going to come true if they keep on," Ruth says.

Blair says the changes in the woods began ... "Well, how old's Dennis?"

Ruth says Dennis is 27.

"Well, Dennis used to help me in the woods, peeling logs, when he was 14, 15, still in high school. I was one of the last ones to peel logs. They weren't clear-cuttin' yet. Even after that, it was a while, then they began saying, 'Cut, cut, cut, cut.'

"I preach husses," Blair says. "With them, you could keep the mills goin' and keep people working in the woods. One man on that Harvester takes the place of 15 men in the woods, and when they ge' done, it's all tore up."

Ruth is sitting nearby on a stool, thinking about the spraying that's about to start. "The governor came on TV and said the paper companies were important and there weren't many people here anyway. Isn't it awful to have a governor who puts paper companies before people? I should think his conscience would bother him when he tries to sleep at night. He gets on the TV and thanks people for conserving gas and leaving it for the tourists. What tourist wants to come to a state that's spraying poison all over them."

"That big green dollar is gonna kill this state," Blair says. "I don't know how they'd get such a product, but if they'd take this money for spray and buy some truth serum and spray it all over Augusta, it'd do more good, I think."

The Yeomanses signed a request form to have their property, where they do organic gardening, exempted from spraying. "They have a line on there that asks what you are concerned about," Ruth says. "They give you examples like bees, cattle, and so on. I wrote in 'People.' They didn't have people on their list.

"Well, I don't say this to be morbid, but we know we don't have a lot longer. We're not worried about ourselves in this. My first thing is children, because we know so little about what it's going to be like for them in 20 years. We have three great-grandchildren and they are so adorable. . . .

"Sometimes I wonder why we're still here when everyone else is gone. My father almost sold this place two times, and we've had fires start. But we stayed. It just seemed we were meant to stay. Maybe something my granddaughter said is a kind of clue. 'Hold onto it, Granny,' she said. 'The way the world's going, we may all be back up there with you.'"

"Blair Yeomans is a true rebel," says Rita Potter, down the road near the one-lane bridge. "He says he'll be out there with a shotgun if they try to spray him, and he says he's going to teach the women to shoot. Says women shoot all wrong."

It sounds like war. "Yes. It is like the war," she says. "First, the spotter comes in, and then there are two or three planes coming in right behind him, spraying poison. You can see the pilots' faces."

She has been with Jim in Wytopitlock for 21 years. "I have been all over the world, and this is the most beautiful place. I felt so lucky to come to this place. But even in 21 years, I have seen it devastated and it breaks my heart because while my daughter may leave here, my son may want to stay where his father's family comes from."

In a federal court in Portland on May 18, a group of citizens and environmental activists tried to stop this year's spraying program, arguing that the sprays may be dangerous, that they are ineffective anyway and that better forest-management programs could eliminate the need for poisons. The judge ruled that the effort came too late, because the planes, the pilots and the poison had arrived in Maine and would have to be paid for. "By the time this case could be properly heard on its merits, the case would be moot," he said.

In the meantime, however, the federal government announced after seeing the Environmental Impact Statement that this is the last year that it will participate in the spraying. The state has also served notice that it wants to get out of the spray project by 1981, leaving the effort to the paper companies, which now pay two-thirds of the cost.

Winds caused delays last week, but on Tuesday evening, as the sky turned golden behind blossoms in the old apple trees behind the dead barns of Wytopitlock, the Alabaman and the rest of Quebec team were in the air, flying out of Old Town airport, laying down a heavy spray on the spruce trees of Aroostook County.

Just about that time a trailer truck pulled out of the yard of a vast paper mill a few miles down the road heading south. The lettering on it side read: "Soften the Blow. Vanity Fair tissue."

AUGUST 5, 1979

DENNYSVILLE, Maine — Betty Ward ran her finger around the edge of a squash leaf whose surface was crinkled like cotton seersucker. She lifted a long, looping tendril of a bean plant and shook her head. "These plants are in agony," she said. "The stuff they sprayed on us is growing them to death."

Her garden, like those of her neighbors in this Maine village of 278 persons, 22 miles northeast of Machias, has been producing mutations since June 30, when a herbicide being sprayed to kill hardwoods in a paper company forest drifted as far as four miles from the target area. The compound Tordon 101, a mixture of 2,4-D and Picloram manufactured by the Dow Chemical Co., fell on gardens, streams, trees, and on people who, unwarned, were working or fishing in the woods being sprayed.

Donald Mairs, secretary of Maine's Pesticides Control Board, called the incident a "disaster . . . the worst I've investigated in the ten years I've been with the Board."

Last week in most of downeast Washington County, produce stands were open along Route 1 to sell summer visitors beet greens, peas, lettuce and soft, fragrant red raspberries. There will be no produce stands in Dennysville this summer. In mid-July, the Maine Departments of Human Services and Agriculture issued a joint statement warning people there not to eat locally grown leafy and pod vegetables. Tordon 101 causes no immediate symptoms such as nausea or vomiting but its components have been found to cause cancer and birth defects in laboratory animals. "We really just don't know the long-term effects of the herbicide," the director of the state's Poison Control Center said.

In Washington, an environmental lobbying organization, Friends of the Earth, has collected research that links 2,4-D and Picloram to cancer. Eric Jansson, a research associate for the group, told the *Journal-Bulletin* Thursday that the combination of chemicals sprayed on Dennysville was the same as that sprayed in the Five Rivers area of Oregon last spring in an incident that he said resulted in miscarriages by five of seven pregnant women there between the end of May and the beginning of July.

As the first month of the disaster ended, Betty Ward and other Dennysville residents walked in their devastated gardens, pointed to squash leaves 20 inches wide, hollyhocks in unprotected areas growing 10-inch leaves in contrast to the three-inch leaves of protected plants, trees that had grown 36 inches in three weeks, tomatoes as big as softballs. They talked with a reporter about their loss, their fears and their anger.

"These were Geneva strawberries," said Mrs. Ward, who with her husband, Blair, owns a 37-acre farm overlooking the Dennys River. The river, said to offer some of the best Atlantic salmon fishing in the country, also collected herbicide that was meant to destroy hardwoods so that pulpwood could flourish on St. Regis Paper Company land. "We had those strawberries eight years and they were wonderful," Mrs. Ward said. "They produce three crops a year; you can't even buy them any more.

"This is asparagus. I planted 50 of these six years ago." As she walked among the neat garden plots, she tallied signs of damage. Tomatoes, potatoes, squash, beans, peas. . . . Dennysville residents have been told that the chemicals will remain in the soil so long that gardens may not be grown until 1981.

"We don't just have a little garden for fun," Mrs. Ward said. "We eat from this garden 365 days a year. We start eating from the garden every year on July 1 and go around the year. I can 44 jars of green beans, 44 jars of wax beans. That takes us through the weeks until the eight weeks when we eat out of the garden. I freeze 80 packages of peas. I haven't bought but one bag of potatoes in four years," she said and went on, almost apologetically, "and that was because mine were getting a little soft and the new potatoes on the market looked good to me. But they didn't taste as good as mine." She looked at the curling, tormented potato leaves of her garden. "Those chemicals should never come near one potato.

"My poor clematis vine got hit. I don't know about the lilacs; it's hard to tell. This could just be bugs; you can't blame everything on the spray. But now look at that! Those are 25-year-old dahlias. Look at those leaves. Now that's not normal. . . . Look at these poor little pink dogwoods I planted this year. I welcomed them to Dennysville."

A towering maple tree shades the Ward's house. "My father planted that tree in 1900. He went down to the woods and dug it up and plunked it right there. Will our hardwoods die?

We don't know. Certainly St. Regis intended to kill theirs. We have 200 wild apple trees on this place; they're just for a deer yard. What will happen to the deer?"

Mrs. Ward looked sharply up at the maple tree. "This is *time* we're talking about. How do you pay for that, I want to know?"

Betty Ward was wearing a button that read, "Question Authority." She wears another that labels her "Protestor Number One," and says, "Yes, I am a protestor. A lot of people won't speak out; it's not the nature of Maine people to be loud-spoken or demanding. But I will say what I think should be said." She was one of those who alerted state officials to the spraying incident, and her sitting room, with its handsome polished Clarion woodstove and comfortable chairs, has become a clearing house for information coming in from Augusta and Washington.

Peggy Rearick of Dennysville came to the Ward's house to report, "My tomatoes have curled, the squash is all mottled and the leaves have changed shape. They're all fan-shaped. The leaves are getting huge."

Betty's husband Sam agreed he'd never seen such leaves. "We'd better start looking for monkeys in there pretty soon," he said.

Sam, who hunts and fishes with Betty, said that paper-company spraying of herbicides to kill hardwoods and of pesticides to kill the spruce budworm is killing wildlife. "There isn't a squirrel in the woods any more. Silent Spring is here. Even the hawks have had to come out of the woods to find anything to eat; there are no little animals in there."

"I was talking to a warden," Betty said, "and he told me that he had found a raccoon in convulsions. He had eaten the frogs that had eaten the bugs that had eaten the poison."

Lee Lingley and his wife, Brenda, finally got a place of their own last September when they bought a little house for themselves and their three boys. You can see the St. Regis land from their place. Lee is a millwright for Georgia Pacific and in the spring, when he hurt his hand, he was able to spend some time working on the first gardens he has ever grown on his own land.

"How I feel about it is I'm p----- off," he said last week. He put on his shoes to take a reporter out to see the gardens that he and Brenda and their oldest boy, seven-year-old John, had planted. He walked up and down the rows, snapping off a pod here, kicking a vine out of the way there. There's a crayoned sign beside one of the garden plots; the signs were everywhere in Dennysville, blackly humorous greetings: "Welcome to Dennysville, home of the droopy pine." "Gas mask area only," this one says. Brenda wrote it. "I'm not a protestor," she said, "but I'm about ready."

"I *have* got a halfway decent garden," Lingley said, accepting a compliment on the plots. "I had 600 linear feet of peas here. Don't dare touch none of it. Just come out here and look at it. When the strawberries were ripe, I had to come out here at night and pick strawberries and throw them away so the two-year-old wouldn't grab them."

Brenda had planned on the garden for winter food. "He hunts and usually gets a deer and he fishes for pollock and, with the garden, that would have given us the winter's food," she said. "I don't know what we'll do to make it now."

Lee snapped off a pod of peas. "These are sugar snap peas. You can eat pods and all. With a certain bravado, he popped a pod of the peas, *his* peas, into his mouth. "Way down deep, I don't believe it would hurt you if you were to cook and eat a mess of peas," he said, "but it might hurt you if you kept on."

"We've had people to say, 'Well, it could have been worse,'" Lingley said. "They've said Skylab could have fallen on us. But I say bull baloney; if Skylab had of fell on us, they would come and pay us to get it back. This way, we may not get anything."

Last week, Maine's Gov. Joseph E. Brennan launched a Cabinet-level investigation of all of the insecticide and herbicide spraying programs in the state, and called St. Regis Paper Co. officials to a closed-door meeting. Three weeks after the incident, St. Regis broke its silence with a three-sentence statement declining to accept responsibility for the Dennysville incident. Responsibility lay with the "independent spraying contractor," the paper company said.

After the meeting with Brennan, St. Regis set up an office in Dennysville. There, residents can present their assessments of damage done to their gardens. An assessor will follow up and if he agrees with the gardeners, checks will be written to those who are willing to sign forms releasing the company from further claims.

"I am telling people not to sign those releases," Betty Ward said. "We have no idea of the damage yet."

"They tell us it will be all right to feed this hay to cattle and that the milk won't hurt anyone," Dana Cox said as he stood between his haybarn and his cowbarn. "Me, I think if there's any chance of harm to people from the milk, I shouldn't have to feed that hay."

The dairy farmer spoke of another warning that people had received in the wake of the spraying. "Somebody asked about burning the wood from the St. Regis land in the woodstoves. A lot of people here get their wood by stumping on that land. They told us that it was only safe to burn the wood if we burned it on a hot fire. That might not work so good early in the morning."

Inside the cowbarn, Cox's red-haired son, Larry, 15, was attaching milking machines to the udders of fat Holsteins. Larry and his uncle, John, and his cousin, Johnnie, were fishing on the St. Regis land on June 30. "My cousin had caught one trout," Larry said. "Then the plane came over and you could feel this mist coming. It settled on the water; it was kind of oily." The man and the boys hurried to leave the woods.

"We came to a St. Regis pickup with three men in it and two other trucks," Larry said. "We asked them for a ride out and they said no, so we started out the fastest way we could." By the time they were clear, the boy said, "they flew right by us about five or six times altogether." The Coxes believe that they were sprayed each time the plane made a pass.

"We called the state police and then called Poison Control and they said take a bath in hot, soapy water."

Larry says that so far, he hasn't felt anything.

Neil and Nellie MacLauchlan aren't afraid of birth defects or cancer so they're going to eat the vegetables in their beautiful garden. Neil is 89 and Nellie is 87. They have lived in the big yellow nineteenth century house for 51 years and for most of those years they have had a garden. "We won't feed them to company and we won't feed them to the grandchildren but it's too good a garden to throw away," Nellie said last week.

She pointed out the flowers she grows in neat rows to attract bees and birds to pollinate the rest of the garden. Not far away, the potatoes are blossoming. "I don't know how much poison could be left in a potato after it's been baked at 450 degrees anyway," she said.

If the MacLauchlans become ill from eating their vegetables, they'll stop, they say, and they do wonder. "When it cripples the leaves like that, you wonder what else it might cripple."

Still, Neil and Nellie say, people are talking mostly about long-term effects and they're serene about those.

"Maybe they need guinea pigs to see what will happen," Mrs. MacLauchlan said. "That's what we'll be."

They came to the front steps to bid the reporter goodbye and to invite her to come back. "But if you read our obituary first," Neil MacLauchlan said, "you'll know what happened."

NOVEMBER 4, 1979

WATERFORD, Conn. — A gull's complaint hung in the air behind Nevio and Diana Petrini's house at Pleasure Beach on Thursday morning. November wind rustled bleached vanilla sea grasses and, just offshore, a lobster boat working traps drew a circle in Niantic Bay. Then the moment was broken by an unsettling rumble from the Millstone nuclear complex, New England's largest nuclear power plant, directly across from the Petrini's back yard. The sound has a primordial depth, like a tearing of the earth.

Nevio looked up from the fishing net he was mending in his back yard. "It was doing that all night last night," he said. "You get used to it. At four o'clock this morning, it scrammed. That's when they have a problem and they shut it down."

During the night, the Millstone II power plant, the second nuclear plant to begin operations since 1970 on Millstone Point across from the pretty Pleasure Beach section of Waterford, was shut down for inspection of cracked welds. Four cracked pipe welds had been discovered during an August inspection ordered by the federal Nuclear Power Regulatory Commission. The plant had reopened after the discovery but it was ordered to close last week for another inspection to see if the cracks had grown, according to a spokesman for Northeast Utilities, owners of the Millstone complex.

"You get used to it," Nevio Petrini said of the noises and the shutdowns.

Two years ago, two explosions within three hours at Millstone released "a slight measurement of radioactivity" and forced the plant closed. A spokesman for the power company said a "gaseous explosion" had blown the door off the base of a chimney that releases radioactive material for the two plants. The spokesman said there had been a minimal discharge of radioactivity accompanied by "a very slight momentary puff of radioactivity."

Last April, it was disclosed that a "low-level" radioactive water leak had occurred a month earlier at the complex 20 miles from Westerly. On March 14, 15,000 gallons of radioactive water overflowed onto the floor of the reactor containment building while employees were correcting a problem with a shut-down cooling pump.

On May 22, Millstone II experienced a breakdown in the automatic reactor protective system.

On June 11, Millstone II was shut down because of a leaking reactor cooling system. Public safety officials said no safety hazard was posed by the radioactive leakage, none of which escaped the containment building. Waterford Fire Marshal Douglas Peabody likened the incident to a kitchen faucet dripping.

The Petrinis and their neighbors are used to such problems. Something that they are not yet used to is a scientist's statement last week that nuclear radiation from the Millstone complex is making Waterford "a dying town." Dr. Ernest Sternglass, professor of radiological physics at the medical school of the University of Pittsburgh, says that his study of cancer rates in the area shows an increase of 12 percent statewide between 1970 and 1975, but an increase of 58 percent in Waterford. He believes that radiation from the Millstone complex is largely responsible.

In a telephone interview on Friday, Sternglass said that he had studied the amount of Strontium 90 and Cesium 130 found in milk and found fallout exceptionally high in the area of the Millstone complex. "In the late 1960s, the trace elements of Strontium 90 and Cesium 130 found in milk were due to atomic bomb tests," he said. "After that, the fallout levels in general kept declining, but the fallout levels in the vicinity of the Millstone kept rising, varying inversely with distance from the plant."

Cancer death rates between 1970 and 1975, taken from Connecticut state statistics, increased between 43 and 44 percent in New London, he said, and 27 percent in New Haven.

Waterford, which lies between Route 95 and Long Island Sound, between New London and the Niantic River, is a bedroom community for New London and Groton. Its main streets have all of the shopping plaza and roadside banking trappings typical of the era, but its smaller streets lead past stone walls, Victorian villages and landscaped parks. Along the waterfront, there are walled estates, subdivisions whose streets are named Albacore or Marlin Drive, homey clusters of bait-and-tackle shops and ice machines and seafood restaurants. Waterford has good schools, an excellent public library, handsome civic buildings.

"It is just about a perfect place to live," Diana Petrini believes.

"I would not live in Waterford, Connecticut," said Ernest Sternglass, "particularly if I were to have children."

Nevio Petrini, who retired from the Army as a lieutenant colonel, built the house for his civilian life on Division Street in Pleasure Beach. He and Diana had traveled the world and settled on this spot, with its crabbing, lobstering, fishing and scalloping, for the good years ahead. A barrier beach just offshore is perfect for the three small grandsons who live nearby; sometimes winters are cold enough to freeze the water behind the sand pit for skating. The air is sea-sweet and the climate so gentle that there's green November lettuce in the Petrinis' garden.

"We started to build about the same time they started to build the plant," Mrs. Petrini said, "but we had no idea how big they were going to get. We thought one plant, but now it's two and they're building a third. At one time, they were even talking about five."

At first, the Petrinis hardly thought about the nuclear complex. It didn't look excessively ugly in the daytime and at night the lights are pretty. When the fog comes in, the plant disappears.

"We weren't afraid. We thought, like everyone, that it would benefit the town," Mrs. Petrini said. "We believed that it was a good neighbor. It was even in the paper that this was one of the safest plants in the country. I think we were brainwashed, to tell the truth."

"While any community would be quick to recognize the tax advantages of such a large operation," the *Evening Bulletin* observed as Millstone I neared completion ten years ago, "not all are as sophisticated as Waterford when it comes to atomic energy." Because many Waterford residents worked on submarines at Groton's Electric Boat shipyard, "they might know that, although nuclear accidents are highly improbable, if there was one, the radioactivity would be contained in the reactor building. . . . They might not know that the 350-foot stack on the site emits radioactive gases, but because they know of the safety precautions required by the Atomic Energy Commission, they would bet the gases would be harmless. The radioactivity in the gases is so slight that the persons living nearest the site would receive less radiation in a year from them than they would on one coast-to-coast flight from cosmic rays."

"When they started building the second one, our feelings began to change," Diana Petrini said last week. "They had several little accidents, and we began to wonder." Relations between Millstone and the surrounding community became slightly chillier as security guards began chasing dog-walking neighbors off the fields that border the plant and ordering squid fishermen away from the warm waters near Millstone point.

"It was hard to take because the water had been for everyone, and now it isn't," Diana Petrini said.

Waterford's tax rate was, indeed, low, but there were those disquieting noises that occasionally awoke the Petrinis. They joked about packing their bags. Then came the accident at Three Mile Island, raising questions about the safety of other plants and deepening the ripple of concern at Pleasure Beach. "No one has ever come to the people who live here and told us, 'Hey. This is what you're supposed to do in case of emergency,'" Petrini said.

"I think they do have a plan," said his wife.

"Well, I don't think they're ever going to put us through a practice," said Nevio. "They'd be afraid they'd scare us to death."

Last week, the Petrinis and their neighbors were talking about the Sternglass report. Nevio summed up his reaction in one sentence: "I'd rather the plant wasn't there."

He and Diana both believe that, as she says, "There is definitely reason for concern about leakage and radiation. The people who run it should know what they're doing, but ever since Three Mile Island, I think everyone is on the cautious side."

"I don't think this plant has been in operation long enough to affect anyone yet," Nevio said. "It wouldn't show up that soon. It might be 15, 20 years before the cancer shows up."

"True," Sternglass told a reporter, "some forms of cancer will not show up for 20 or 25 years, but some skin cancers and leukemia can appear in two or three years. The peak of Hiroshima's cases occurred five years after the atomic bomb blast. Lymph cancer can appear fast; pancreatic cancers might take five to seven years, lung cancer 10 to 12 years."

Assertions in Sternglass's report were disputed by Connecticut's chief health statistician, who called the Waterford cancer rate no different from the rate in Connecticut as a whole. "The (Sternglass) figures are correct and accurate, but invalid because they are not appropriate for use in comparing anything," said Dr. Merton Honeyman, director of the Connecticut Department of Health Services' Division of Health Statistics. "These are crude death rates and crude death rates don't mean anything. He misuses the data in that he picks data that will support his contentions."

Gary Doughty, nuclear information officer for Northeast Utilities, disagreed with Sternglass's use of data from 1970 and 1975. Sternglass said he used those two years because one marked the first year of operation at Millstone and one was five years later. But Doughty said, "The numbers fluctuate. He picked those two years and got an increase."

"We are very concerned about (the issues raised by Sternglass)," Diana Petrini said. "Not so much for ourselves as for our children and grandchildren. My daughter feels very strongly about the health of her children — no chemicals in the food, everything natural. But the poison can reach them through the air."

Would they ever consider leaving? "Not me. I intend to stay here until I die," Nevio said.

"I would just hate to leave, but of course if we had to . . ." Diana said. "If we came down with something, we might have to."

On Thursday at Pleasure Beach, there were swans in the water and gulls in the air. Across the way, seven cranes hung above the construction site of Millstone III. Behind the house at 23 Division St., Nevio Petrini was mending his net. Next door, a new house is being built for a couple who will be able to move in just about the time their baby is born.

DECEMBER 9, 1979

MARBLEHEAD, Mass. — Steve Zardis' telephone sits on an end table littered with file folders and notepads. Notes in a loose, childish hand, written as Zardis talks to strangers who have called him, overflow the pages.

"Maybe they've read a story in the morning paper and it has taken them all day to call. They'll say, 'I get this numbness in my hands and sometimes I drop tools . . .' Or they'll say, 'I was in Vietnam and my baby was born deformed. Do you think there's any connection?' Those are the worst calls. 'My baby was born with a bladder outside his body,' or 'My baby was born with two sets of sex organs. I was reading about the effects of Agent Orange . . .' "

Stephen J. Zardis, who has been told that he may have as little as two years before "I'm a vegetable lying on my back staring up at the ceiling," intends to use the rest of his time, and whatever money he can squeeze from his disability checks, to arouse public awareness of the dangers of the chemical herbicide 2,4,5-T, which, mixed with 2-4-D, is known as Agent Orange. The defoliant was heavily used by the United States in Vietnam and is still in use on rangelands and rice fields in this country.

Last March 1, the Environmental Protection Agency announced an emergency ban on all uses of the herbicide 2,4,5-T on forestlands, pastures and utility and railroad rights of way in the United States because of dangers to human health from a highly toxic contaminant, a dioxin, contained in the chemical.

Many studies have found the dioxin to have severe toxic effects, including miscarriages and birth defects.

"The toxin gets into the ecosystem, into the water table, and that's where the problems arise," Zardis, the Massachusetts veteran, said. "It has been shown that it gets into the fatty tissue of cattle and some scientists think that's what's happening to us, that the poison is there, stored in our bodies."

Zardis is director of the Massachusetts chapter of Agent Orange Victims International, which he runs alone from his apartment and finances from his disability check and an occasional unsigned letter enclosing a few dollars. He suffers from a degenerative neurological disorder that Veterans Administration doctors have diagnosed as "acute, atypical multiple sclerosis" but that he believes is a result of exposure to Agent Orange during the year and a day he spent in the Army in Vietnam.

"Basically, I have a serious neurological deterioration of the nervous system, exhibiting itself in severe tremors and all kinds of unpleasantness," Zardis explains with no trace of pathos.

He is one of several named plaintiffs in a class-action suit pending in U.S. District Court in Westbury, N.Y., against five chemical firms that produced the defoliant: Dow, Monsanto,

Hercules, Diamond-Shamrock, and Thompson-Hayward. "You don't sue the dealer who *sold* you the Pinto," he observed last week as he spoke with a reporter at his ground-floor apartment near Marblehead harbor. The suit grew out of action originally taken by the family of the founder of Agent Orange Victims International, Paul Reutershan, who died of cancer a year ago.

"We want to get the chemical out of production throughout the world," Zardis said. "We want a trust fund established to study the problems of the veterans. It needs to be studied now. And we want veterans to get treatment or compensation for treatment they have received. In my case, the government would be reimbursed for the costs of my care."

Lawyers who are representing the veterans in the suit believe that as many as 300,000 American veterans and their children may suffer ill effects of the fathers' exposure to the defoliant.

Zardis' own story, which he tells as dispassionately as if he were reading from a file — "I don't have enough time left to get angry" —began when he enlisted in the Army in 1967. He was a student at Boston College, a healthy athlete and a member of the wrestling team. "Most people were still behind the war then. It wasn't that I was rushing off to kill a Commie for Christ or anything, but I had lost quite a few friends from high school. I just felt that I was an, ah, able-bodied, ah, citizen in a country where they needed able-bodied citizens to help fight the war."

He was in Vietnam from April, 1968, to April, 1969. "I had some subtle symptoms while I was there, but you overlook them. It was a decrepit part of the world. We lived in filth. In view of the general health conditions out there, it wasn't a surprise to have skin problems, urinary difficulties."

He was treated for a number of such ailments while in Vietnam, where he served in Military Region III, the sector from Saigon northwest to the Cambodian border. Zardis says he has learned that U.S. planes sprayed more gallons of Agent Orange on Region III than on any other area in Vietnam. "Nobody paid much attention to the spraying out there," he said. "We thought it was for pest control."

The Government Accounting Office, at the request of Illinois Sen. Charles Percy, examined Defense Department figures on herbicide spraying in Vietnam and reported recently that the department's contention that no U.S. troops entered areas contaminated with Agent Orange for six weeks after spraying was "inaccurate." The GAO report suggested that Congress direct a government study of the effects of Agent Orange on those who served in Vietnam. Senator Percy and California Sen. Alan Cranston have co-sponsored a bill calling for a study by the Department of Health, Education and Welfare, which they feel would be more objective than Defense or the VA.

Until now, no overall study has been done. The only study of former military personnel now under way is being conducted by the Air Force, which carried out the spraying in a program called Operation Ranch Hand, renamed from Operation Hades.

"I think I have pretty well adjusted to the fact that there is no cure for me," Steve said. He sat in his wheelchair, smoking Camels as he supported one shaking wrist with the other hand. "I am not doing this because I hope to be cured. I want to get the government to face up to this question and do an immediate study. I am thinking about the well-being of the veterans and of the children who are being born. The typical Vietnam veteran is now in his late 20s, early 30s, the age when they will be having their families. We can't wait 10 or 20 years to find out."

When Steve came back from Vietnam, he finished college on the GI Bill and became a social worker. The first signal that something was wrong with his health came from his thumb, which lost sensation. "Between the spring of 1976 and the winter of 1977, I went from numbness in one hand to numbness in both hands and then in both feet. By the summer of 1977, I had to use a cane. By winter, I was wearing braces."

The VA diagnosed his illness as multiple sclerosis, "but my case was not typical. It is not usual for it to progress so rapidly. So they called it 'atypical multiple sclerosis.' It was just coincidental that I had served in the area of Vietnam most heavily sprayed with Agent Orange.

"Still, I kept questioning myself, 'How come I'm going so quickly?' The typical pattern is one of remission followed by exacerbation, but I have had no remissions. They keep saying I'm bound to have one soon."

Some symptoms of exposure to Agent Orange may be markedly similar to those of multiple sclerosis, Zardis said. Agent Orange Victims International supplies veterans with lists of symptoms and effects that have been found in victims of accidents in plants producing Agent Orange in this country and abroad. The list begins with chloracne (skin eruptions on face, neck and back; numbness in extremities; nerve damage; fatigue; nervousness; irritability; intolerance to cold; palpable and tender liver; insomnia; loss of sex drive; dizziness and shortness of breath), and goes on through 12 others that may be experienced by the person who has been exposed to the chemical, as well as seven birth deformities and four forms of cancer.

"The VA does not recognize dioxin poisoning as a service-connected liability. It is the opinion of our organization that the VA must recognize the suffering, death and deformed children born to Vietnam veterans as a result of being exposed to Agent Orange," Zardis' organization tells veterans who contact them. (The Massachusetts chapter, closest to Rhode Island, is at 18 Merritt St., Marblehead, Mass. 09145. Telephone is 617-631-0512.)

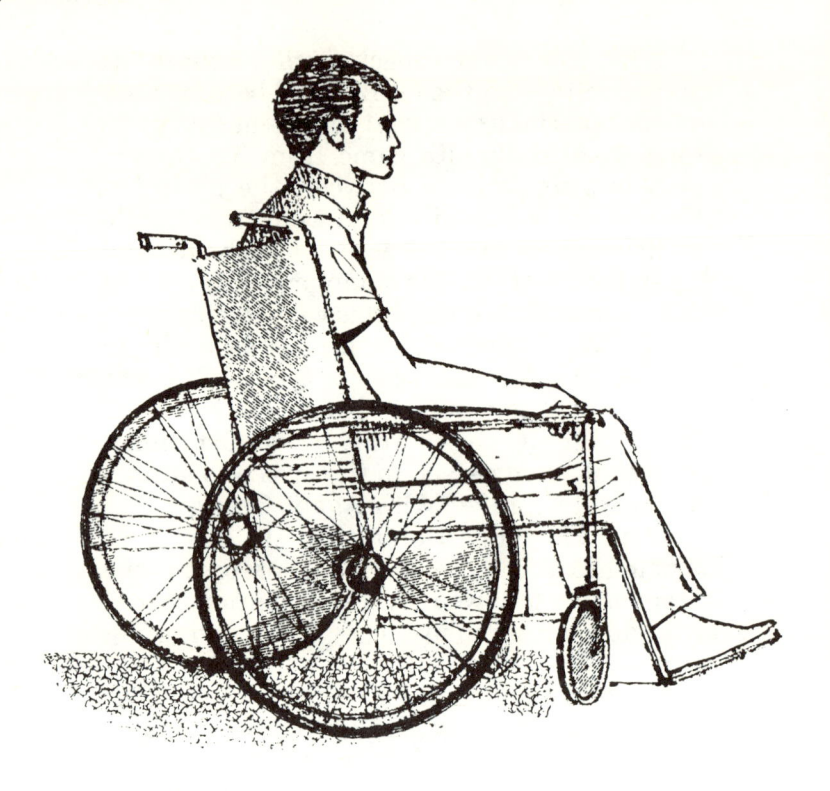

A VA spokesman in Washington said last week that the agency has a total of 750 Agent Orange claims currently "under study."

"People don't want to hear about Vietnam any more," Steve said. He yanked at one of his Adidas Nastase tennis shoes, pulled his foot into place on the wheelchair's footrest. "Everybody wants it to go away. I call it benign malevolence. You go to government officials and they rub their heads, 'Oh, yes, the Vietnam veteran,' and sigh.

"The media aren't interested. They said, 'We already did our piece on the Vietnam vets,' or 'Geraldo Rivera already did that.'"

Steve began to do research on Agent Orange in the spring of 1978. "I had complete trust in my doctors; they said, 'You have MS. You have acute, atypical MS.' One doctor became a good friend. He said, 'Look, officially, you have MS. But as your friend, I think you should look into other possibilities.'

"Then I read an article on Servaso, Italy." Servaso was the Lombard town where a factory explosion in July, 1976, produced a cloud of dioxin that affected people in nearby communities who developed nausea, eye and throat irritations, dizziness, headaches, burn-like sores and other symptoms. The article read by Zardis reported on the similarities between these symptoms and those experienced by civilians who had been exposed to Agent Orange in Vietnam and Cambodia. He came to believe there is a connection between his illness and his exposure to defoliants in Vietnam.

"I can't substantiate it medically, but neither can anyone refute it," he says. "That's why we're trying to get a thorough study done."

The Vietnam veterans have a vague sense of guilt about their war and themselves, Zardis says. Like most parents, they feel some personal guilt when a deformed child is born to them. When some have read that the child's deformity may be related to a chemical they had no control over, they have called Steve Zardis. "Or they write, and say thank you for what you're doing. They say that it is a relief to them to have someone speak up who is an articulate person with a definite goal in mind. Sometimes, somebody will put a couple of dollars in the envelope and just write, 'Thanks.' That's what I mean when I say I haven't got time to be angry. I have to keep working as long as I can.

"We know one thing for sure. There is something wrong with the Vietnam veteran. More of us have died since the end of the war than were killed in combat. Our health is not very good. We'd like to know why."

DECEMBER 23, 1979

GRAY, Maine — As the week ended, houses around "The Triangle," the section east of town formed by Route 115, Mayall Road and Depot Road, were decorated for Christmas. Cheryl Washburn has woven holiday macrame to hang in her doors and windows, and the tree was up at Cathy Hinds' house.

Everywhere you looked there were cheery lights and cut-out Clauses to make the season fun for the children. At the Wink farmhouse up Depot Road, an old sideboard holds a hoard of wrapped parcels. Everyone is looking forward to Christmas, but most agreed that the holiday would be more fun if everybody felt better.

Cathy's four-year-old daughter Jamie was feeling kind of croupy and listless. She whined and sniffled and clung to her mother. In a house near the closed-up, fenced-in McKin Co. pit, Linda Fusco was feeling terrible. She opened a bedroom window to speak to a visitor who knocked at her back door. "I have been feeling bad as long as I can remember," she said, "since that time I had the kidney trouble. I can't seem to feel good. Now I've got to go to the doctor to have a couple of things checked. I've got a growth on my tongue.... I don't want to go to the doctor because I'm kind of worried what he'll tell me."

George and Cheryl Washburn are popping Excedrin like M & Ms, and Greg Hinds still has the asthma that came on a couple of years ago. Coffee goes right through Cathy; she has to go to the bathroom after even one cup. People in East Gray are getting used to feeling below par, but it's too bad to feel that way at Christmas.

The trouble at Gray began in 1972, years before Kevin Washburn or Melissa and Jamie Hinds or their baby brother who died were even born. That year, the *Tamano,* a Norwegian tanker chartered by Texaco, ran into a ledge outside of Portland harbor and spilled 100,000 gallons of heavy industrial oil into the Bay. People in Gray don't remember now exactly how it happened.

The oil, solvents and oil-soaked seaweed were cleaned up and trucked to the McKin Co. pit on Mayall Road in East Gray, owned by Richard Dingwell, who has always lived in town. A man who once ran for public office here, Dingwell has not made any public statements in the last two years, on the advice of his lawyer. Nearly eight years ago, his McKin Co. received an emergency permit through an agreement with the town and the Maine Department of Environmental Protection to dispose of the *Tamano* waste by burning it in an approved incinerator.

In September, 1972, as the incinerator went into operation. Dingwell said he was "tickled to death" with the operation. No one seems to have noticed that some time later, Dingwell stopped burning the waste and began simply dumping it. Nor did anyone notice when the pit took on new customers — clients with chemicals to dump. Nor had anyone, before the permit was granted, tested the town's gravel aquifer to study the dump's potential effect on well water in the area.

The well water smelled bad by 1973. Patrick and Bertha Sullivan, who lived on Mayall Road, started carrying drinking water from outside East Gray because theirs smelled so bad. They kept using it for washing and cooking, but you couldn't drink the stuff.

"I hope your water is better than mine," Pat Sullivan told young Cheryl Washburn when she moved into Mayall Road in 1975. The Qualey subdivision was attracting young couples who were ready for their first houses. Cheryl and her husband, George, who is a salesman for York Biscuit at Biddeford, wanted to move to the country.

The Washburns financed their house through the Farmers Home Administration, which provides loans to build homes in rural areas to low- and moderate-income families that are "without decent, safe, and sanitary housing."

After they moved in, Cheryl discovered that her water, too, smelled bad, had a kind of rotten-egg smell. "From the time we moved in, you couldn't get it past your nose," she says. "I went up to Farmers Home and took a sample of the water. It was all slimy. I asked the number-two man there if they could test my water and he said, 'I don't know how to read a water analysis.'"

"Cheryl was bumming water off me," says the Washburn's neighbor, Cathy Hinds, laughing wryly, because of what they learned later about *her* water. "I didn't really notice the smell of mine at first because, being a city girl from Portland, I was used to Sebago Lake water and I thought all well water had an odd smell to it."

Cathy's daughter Melissa was born two months after she moved to East Gray; Cheryl was pregnant that first year in the new house. The two women became close friends right away, and after all they have been through, facing the annoyance of the town and standing up to government officials, each has sometimes felt like the other's only friend.

Cathy's water didn't smell at first, but as the water trouble spread, hers, too, "had a stink, not like rotten eggs, but more like my septic tank was backing up into my house."

Cheryl took a sample of her water to Gray's town health officer, Robert J. McNally, who sent it off to the state for testing. When Pat Sullivan heard that it was being tested, he took McNally some reports he had received when he had sent samples of his water off to the same lab. Several tests had told him the water was safe, but on one report, a handwritten note read, "two highly volatile substances." When McNally spotted that, he recalled later in an interview with a Portland *Express* reporter, he told the state water-quality lab, "no more tests for iron, zinc, coliform or anything like that. Find out what in hell those two highly volatile substances are."

After three months, the state said its equipment could not give the answer. A second lab was tried; it was the first of a series of facilities that would spend nearly two years coming up with an answer to the question about East Gray water.

In 1976, Timmy Washburn got a brother. Kevin was born.

The water seemed to be getting worse. By that fall, even Cathy realized that her water was smelling. "It had happened so gradually that I didn't notice, but I had company from out of state and they said, 'Cathy, your water stinks.'"

By then, showers stung bathers' skin, and the wash was coming out with black, oily spots on it. In some houses, the shower tiles and the insides of the dishwashers were turning black. More and more people began noticing the trouble, which seemed to be spreading out through the Qualey subdivision. Hauling water became a regular part of life for most families by choice. The outside water was used for drinking, but in most houses you could boil the well water and use it for cooking and not notice a taste or smell, and everybody kept using the well water for washing.

In November of that Bicentennial year, Paul Noonan, who works for the Maine Department of Human Services as an industrial hygienist, responded to a call from McNally and visited Gray. "He went into my bathroom," Cheryl remembers, "and he was gagging when he came out. He just said, 'Whew!'"

Noonan wondered if the smell might be coming from a natural-gas line that runs through the area, and he sent samples to the University of Maine, which reported the contamination was unrelated to natural gas.

In January, 1977, Noonan heard about Energy Resources Co., a sophisticated laboratory in Cambridge, Mass. ERCO's preliminary analysis, showing the presence of two chemicals in East Gray water, arrived in April. Four months later, ERCO told McNally that seven of the 11 wells that had been tested by then were dangerously contaminated and recommended that the water not be used for cooking or drinking.

In November, a consulting firm reported the presence of other chemicals and suggested it would be "prudent to discontinue pumping these wells." Its report also recommended discontinuing the use of the water for drinking, bathing and cooking.

By the end of 1977, the people of East Gray knew most of the contaminants in their water, a list that ultimately included trichloroethane, trichloroethylene, xylene, benzene, carbon tetrachloride, methylene chloride, dimethylsilanol, dimethylsulfide, acetone, freon, alcohols, toluene and dibromomethane.

Six of the chemicals are central-nervous-system poisons that can cause headaches, fatigue, nausea, giddiness, loss of coordination, and depression. Some of the chemicals can affect the peripheral nervous system and cause numbness. Some are known cancer-causers. Secondary effects from the poisons can include increased chance of infection, tiredness, and bleeding problems.

In September, 1977, the McKin operation on Mayall Road, which soil samples had identified as the source of the contamination, was ordered closed. Beneath the gravel was an aquifer, an underground layer of water-filled gravel into which the Triangle's wells were drilled. For five years, a deadly broth of chemicals had been leaking into that aquifer and finally, through the wells, the kitchens and bathrooms of Qualey subdivision. A U.S. Environmental Protection Agency study showed that between 100,000 and 200,000 gallons of oil, septic tank and industrial wastes had been processed each year the McKin pit was in operation.

Later, investigators who went to the closed site found a small pond containing oily liquid, oil on the ground eight to 12 inches deep. Large holding tanks were rusted and corroded. Chemical drums, some of them open or uncapped, were scattered around the surface. A surface cleanup was carried out, but the cost of cleaning the chemicals from beneath the surface was prohibitive. What was cleaned up from the McKin pit was trucked to Massachusetts.

(The search for approved or even unapproved dumping spots for chemicals goes on. Greg Hinds, who works for the Maine Turnpike Authority, said last week that a truck of hazardous waste had been stopped on the turnpike by a trooper who wanted to check a license plate. "The truck was carrying sand and it was from Massachusetts," Hinds said. "He got to thinking, why would anybody haul sand from Massachusetts all the way to Maine when Maine's got plenty of sand of its own? He looked underneath and it was chemicals. The guy was going to dump 'em.")

By the fall of 1977, Pat and Bertha Sullivan, who had been carrying their water for four years, were told to stop cooking with the well water, but continued to use it for washing clothes. They had to go outside when the washing machine was running because the smell was so bad.

Cathy Hinds, who had been bleeding heavily, miscarried in the third month of pregnancy. People in town complained of rashes and dizziness, listlessness and headaches. Cheryl and Cathy did a telephone survey to determine the extent of it. "It was housewife data," Cheryl says, comfortable now with scientists' jargon, "but just listening to them on the phone, I almost cried. It was just too much in this one little place to be coincidence."

Listing the results of that survey for a reporter in her kitchen, Cathy read, "Of 11 homes, seven reported skin rashes, five reported eye irritations, four mentioned urinary-tract problems, seven reported symptoms of central-nervous-system disorders: fatigue, depressions, loss of equilibrium, loss of coordination." She excused herself for a moment, because of the cup of coffee she had just finished, and when she returned, she continued, "Other symptoms were temporary blindness, numbness in extremities, listlessness. Eight reported gastro-intestinal problems; three reported respiratory problems. There has been one miscarriage and one neonatal death."

"That was *my* son," said Greg Hinds, who sat across the table from his wife.

Cathy had been ill throughout her pregnancy in 1978. "I bled the whole time," she says. "In March, I suffered from exhaustion and numbness in my arms and legs. In September, I blacked out from dizziness."

Gregory Hinds, the baby boy who was born a year ago today, died two days later, on Christmas morning. "The hospital told us that his kidneys had failed," Cathy said.

In January, 1978, most of the wells of Qualey subdivision were capped and the town began hauling water into Qualey subdivision, but the contamination was spreading. "It got into the aquifer and it reached the waterways and began to move along them," says Eska Wink, who lives on Depot Road beyong the Triangle. Like many people in the community, she speaks of the poison as "it," a malevolent presence. "It has gone right down Collyer Brook. Collyer brook flows into the Royal River. It was scary, knowing it was coming. We had been in our house for about a year and a half when this came up and there was nothing we could do."

In the Wink's old farmhouse the sun blazed through the windows decorated with doily snowflakes. Inside, 13-year-old Ellen played with two white kittens. "My husband works in Portland and he hauled water in the truck until we had the water piped in," Mrs. Wink recalled. "There was a lot of inconvenience — bathing, for example. They opened up the high school for showers, but that wasn't like being at home. We had a pony and we had to give it away because we couldn't haul enough water for a pony. You learned not to cook some things — spaghetti, for instance — that take a lot of water."

Why did people stay? For one thing, as Cheryl Washburn found when she called a real-estate agent, the affected houses were suddenly worthless. "I asked the agent how much she could get me for my house and she said, 'Nothing.' What can you do? We don't have enough money for two houses."

"Even if you could find a buyer, you could not morally sell to someone else," Mrs. Wink said. The people of East Gray are, as Cathy Hinds says, prisoners in their houses. "Even if we could move," Cheryl Washburn says, "we don't know, we might be taking the problem with us. It may already be in our bodies and our children's and could appear years from now, somewhere else."

In December, 1977, Pat and Bertha Sullivan did move, to Poland Spring. Pat, who was then 64, said that he had been hauling water for four years and seven months and was suffering from back trouble and infections. He had had it with East Gray.

That month, two years ago, the wells of East Gray were ordered capped after a case of kidney trouble in the family of Fernando and Linda Fusco of Mayall Road. Although newspapers reported that it was Kelly Fusco, then nine, who was taken to the emergency room of Mercy Hospital with bladder and liver trouble, Kelly's mother, Linda, says that was an error. "I was the one who had the trouble, and I haven't felt good since then." McNally, the health officer, warned that well water should not even be used for flushing toilets because of toxic fumes.

After a period when water was trucked to East Gray, town water was extended to the community. In August, 1978, a ceremony was held at the Washburn's house to turn the water on. George was working but Cheryl was there to welcome Maine Sen. William Hathaway and the mayor of Lewiston. Hathaway ceremoniously turned on the town water and Cheryl did not tell him that the water had been on for several days. She made a speech of thanks, the officials went away and as far as Cheryl knows, no one in the Triangle has ever heard a word from any of them since.

State officials and federal representatives have not been as visible at East Gray as they have been at Love Canal. Cheryl says, for instance, that she has never heard from her representative in Congress, does not even know his name.

"After we got the water, people in Gray thought we ought to be satisfied," Cheryl Washburn observed recently. But the health problems persisted, and Cheryl and Cathy felt something should be done about them. "I wonder if the chemicals could have knocked out the defense against infection. My son has had pains when he urinates, and my husband and I have had so many ailments."

"I am determined to raise public consciousness of chemical-waste dumping," says Cathy, who says when this all began she didn't know what the term hazardous chemical meant. "People in this town, if you want to know the truth of it, can't stand the sight of Cheryl and me. We're bringing down real-estate values with our big mouths. But I have these awful scares, an image of a generation of deformed American children."

Last spring, Cathy and Cheryl testified at the state capitol about the need for legislation dealing with hazardous waste disposal, and Cathy spoke of her miscarriage and the death of her baby boy. Her testimony was heard by a consultant in environmental health planning, who was surprised to learn from the women that no follow-up health study had been done at Gray.

He contacted Dr. Beverly Paigen, a health research scientist at Roswell Park Memorial Institute in Buffalo, N.Y., who had worked with victims at Love Canal. In that community, Dr. Paigen reported finding an abnormal number of kidney and bladder ailments and problems of the reproductive system. An unusual number of miscarriages, birth defects, nervous breakdowns, cases of epilepsy, and high rates of hyperactivity and suicide were noted.

After Dr. Paigen visited Gray, she wrote a letter this October urging Maine officials to carry out a detailed health questionnaire, a physical exam, and to follow them with a yearly repeat of the questionnaire and physical exam if necessary for the next five years. Comparing

East Gray and Love Canal on the basis of just one of the chemicals found at both sites, she said that an adult in Gray could have taken in 30 times more trichloroethylene in one day than a person in Love Canal.

Measuring the effects of the poisons on the residents of East Gray may not be enough, she said, because the chemicals are still in the aquifer. She warned that there is possibility of further leakage from still-buried material into the aquifer because only the surface has been cleaned.

Then there is the question of toxic fumes. At Love Canal, well water was not the cause of illness; toxic fumes, produced by some of the same combinations of chemicals found at Gray, were. Dr. Paigen recommended that air tests be made in cellars to see if the chemicals are moving through the soil at East Gray as they did at Love Canal. Two weeks ago, tests for toxic fumes were made for the first time in six houses of Qualey subdivision. "We don't know if we're breathing fumes. A person has the right to know if they are breathing poison," Cathy Hinds said as the neighborhood waited for a report.

"If the report shows fumes, I don't know what we'll do," Cheryl Washburn said. "My folks have a place in Turner. I guess we could. . . . I couldn't live here any more. I couldn't. As far as my children's health, I feel I have already done something awful to them."

She looked out her kitchen window toward Greg and Cathy's house. "Christmas is going to be awful. We'll all be remembering last year, the baby. We sat here all day thinking about them and then I said to George. 'We've got to go over there. Let's take them a dinner.' We put a dinner for them in a cooler and carried it over. It was snowing. . . ."

"The worst thing is, it will be here for 200 years," said Eska Wink. "There's just no way to neutralize it. And I have the feeling that we're just the tip of the iceberg nationwide. They've been burying chemicals from here to East Overshoe, Idaho, for years, with no thought to the future. Somebody has to start worrying about where all this stuff is going."

EPILOGUE: Last week, the six East Gray families whose air had been tested for "outgassing" of trichloroethylene fumes from the soil received copies of the state Health Engineering Division's report. Traces of the compound were found in the air at the homes of Frederick Cartwright, Donald Cormier, and Fernando Fusco, but the report stressed that the amounts found were "well over 6,000 times lower than what is acceptable in a workplace." No trace of the chemical was found in the air at the Washburn or Hinds homes or the residence of Nathaniel Greene. Cheryl Washburn asked if the state would do follow-up tests to see if more of the fumes are detected with the passage of time.

"They told me that was a good idea," she says.

CONVERSATIONS

CLARK: Did you conceive of these stories as a series?

McCABE: No. Each was absolutely spontaneous. When I did the Wytopitlock piece, I had no notion that we'd be dealing with the shutdown at Millstone or the guy with the disease he blamed on Agent Orange. But it turned out that environmental stories were the big stories last year. We felt that these stories were as important in their way as Three Mile Island because they were perhaps harbingers of what's going to be coming everywhere. It doesn't have to be a devastating disaster like TMI. It could be a little thing like spray drifting in your garden.

What kind of stories are you dealing in here? What's your specialty?

I'm not doing stories about the economy or about institutions or about the environment. I'm doing people stories. This is something that Joel Rawson (managing editor) and I feel strongly about. The news right now seems not to be what somebody in the Federal Reserve Board or what the President says in his speech tonight or what battle was won. The news seems to be coming out of the changes happening in the lives of people, very much as it was in the 30s. In its simplest form this is "walk and talk." We try to get at people's feelings about the economy, about their expectations for their kids, about how they're scared in the grocery store because of inflation. We did a story about what it is that makes people stand in that checkout line chewing their lower lips and acting very jumpy. And if a kid comes up with a package of potato chips that's not on the list, they smack the kid. There's something going on, but it's inside people and you have to bring it out and give it shape.

I'm interested in how a story develops on this people beat. Does somebody say to you "We

hear that someone's growing monster tomatoes in Maine"?

The monster tomato story is not perhaps the best example. That was a given place, a small town. The logical thing was that you went there and talked to everyone whose tomatoes were monsters. It was easy to find them. Maybe a better one is the budworm stories which involved the whole state of Maine. Joel knew about this massive spraying program. He was a pilot in Vietnam and he said "There's something there, go on up and see what you can find out." Maine is a rather large state to "go see what you can find out." In this case I started out with the court action. I went to cover a hearing. From that I worked backwards, asked where the spraying was taking place. I went to that little town where most of these spray planes were based, hung around there, hung around the motel, talked to people, went in and sat in a pilots' meeting. I found out where on the map the spraying was taking place, went into the area and began searching out people who were affected.

How did you know which people to develop the story around?

Something happens with me that I hesitate to put a label on. I don't know quite what it is. It's like people who have ESP or something they can't define. I know there's something I have that a lot of other reporters don't have, which is a kind of sense of who's going to be good. I can pick, as in the Waterford story, about where the right street is going to be. I don't mean to make this sound like some kind of cosmic thing. It's my own built-in geiger counter.

Once you find them, how do you bring these people to life for your readers?

I'm writing stories. I'm using them as characters in stories. They're telling their own stories. They come to life because they are alive, and I try to employ language skillfully so they are not just pieces of type.

Most of us are into working with characters in the same way that fiction writers do.

I notice that you try to give a sense of the peculiar character of a person's language by including verbal pauses or regional features.

I think the American language is pure poetry. We fall into two opposing camps here. I feel very strongly that it is condescending to make everyone sound as if they're speaking Standard English when they are not. I think their speech is just as good as any I could make up for them. I'm not trying to make it ungrammatical or make them sound stupid. I'm trying to let the poetry of the life they've led, the experiences they've had, come out through the rhythms of the speech.

You have some wonderful, long quotes in your stories. How do you get it all?

I take notes. Do you know Denis Brian's book about interviewing the interviewers? It's very good. It's called *Murderers and Other Friendly People* (McGraw, 1973). When he talked to Gay Talese, he said "It's extraordinary that you get these quotes, do people really talk this way, are they real quotes?" And Talese answered "Nobody has ever come to me and said 'This isn't me.'" And I think that's the only proof.

What are some of your interviewing techniques?

I've developed a system which seems to work for me. I take down key words, and if there are unusual patterns of speech I write these down exactly, and I have what I can only refer to as a tape recorder in my head. When I go back to the notes, I hear the voices again in my head. From the key words I can hear them speaking. And I would rather use a notebook and use eye contact and be free to work with body language than use a tape recorder. The kind of people I write about most I feel I would be intruding on our relationship with a mechanical device. And there's always the specter of disaster if the machine doesn't work.

How do you work with body language?

I interpret body language for myself, to try to tell the mood of the person. I also use it to help with the interview, and I'm sure you know these techniques. You work into the interview gradually, watching to see if they're feeling more at ease, particularly when they start to echo your posture, and you begin to test. You're sitting there with your arms folded. If I suddenly did the same thing unconsciously, you'd know that we're very close and that you could then ask an important question.

I think interviewing is one of the most intimate relationships whether you do it in a small closed room or in a corner of a big hall. There's an electricity flowing between the two people. When you really get into it, it becomes a physical thing, almost a sexual attraction.

How do you reconcile the crafts of reporting and writing?

It's the reporting that underlies the good writing. You've got to have the basic facts to build on, and then you work with language in a way that makes it not "fancier" — I like "plainer." John McPhee says he spends hours looking through dictionaries for the perfect word, which is not a polysyllabic, Roman-root word, but a nice pithy Anglo-Saxon square plain word that gives you a picture.

How does the reporting contribute to your writing?

By reporting how it was. You ask the questions: What was it like? What did it feel like? Take the reader where he cannot go. You, reporter, go in and bring back information. What is it like in those woods? What is it like on that island? What is it like in that person's dreams? And you do that by accumulating every bit of meaningful detail and using it where it seems appropriate. It's what you leave out sometimes that is as important as what you put in.

Do you write quickly?

I have to. We may talk about a story on Monday, line up a plane or rental car and get the photographer on Tuesday, come back on Thursday, so I have to write on Friday for the story to run Sunday. So I write very intensely for that one day, and so often I'll read the story on Sunday and say "Good Lord, I left out my best quote, or an anecdote, and if I had two weeks I'd do it better." But it isn't worth two weeks. You've got another story next week. It's just the nature of the business. Another problem with the writing. I love the A-TEXT computer terminals—the shortening of the time between the thought and the reproduction of the thought is remarkable—but we don't have enough to go around. So on Friday everyone is fighting for a terminal, hanging on for dear life and not going to the john lest somebody take your machine. The result is an intense day of writing.

Let's say you come back with a pile of notes for a story. What happens then? I want to get some sense of the process.

I go through my notes and put the most important material into the machine, sorting the material by categories and groups of thoughts and chronology. I will usually see where I'm going to add my statistical material, background facts, quotes from governmental officials. Then I will run a printout of my notes and begin to mark that up. An arrow here. A transition here. A question mark there. The usual little roadmap. I know by then where the lead is and I sit down and write the lead and the story comes tumbling after.

Do you rewrite much?

Yes. Perhaps every time I get a full screen I'll go back and rewrite for grace and rhythm. Joel says that occasionally I'll read with my lips moving. I'm doing that because I'm hearing it. I'm writing for the ear. Someday somebody should do a study of how people work at these terminals because each one has his own rhythm. We've got one guy who plays the piano. He sits down as if he were Liberace, and he sort of rocks with it as if he's hearing an inner music.

I have a question about objectivity. I sense a writer who is sensitive to the plight of the people she's writing about. I'm sure some people might criticize you for not being detached enough.

I don't want to fall into the sob sister category, but I love seeing what people do when they're in corners, grace under pressure, how people behave when the chips are down. That's my favorite story. I believe that there is not as much objectivity possible in journalism as some observers feel, because as long as you have human beings selecting facts that are used, it comes through a subjective mind. A reporter expressing his feelings should never replace the plain statement of fact, but I think we need people who will go and try to explain what is beyond those facts. I think Eudora Welty described the writing process in terms of the Old Bards. The King died and then the Queen died. That's narrative. The King died and then the Queen died of grief. That's plot. Maybe what we're talking about is narrative and plot, and what I'm trying to do is put some plot in the story.

I know if I gave these stories to a group of editors, I'd probably hear some complain that the nut graph or the significance graph is too far down in the story, especially in the first one. It takes you eight paragraphs to get to the point.

That sounds like J-school talk to me. This is an idiosyncrasy. Joel tears his hair, and sometimes he's been reduced to putting the point or the nut in the caption under the picture. I don't like sticking it in, out of place, out of rhythm. Maybe this is self-indulgence. I just want people to get interested in the story and to go with it. I want them to read it because it's readable, and to come to the point naturally.

Maybe the point isn't what I think it is: It seems more natural to me to write a gradual narrative. Faulkner doesn't give you the plot in the first sentence.

Aren't your stories a bit long? Should newspaper stories be that long?

People read books, don't they. Maybe they don't bring that same commitment to the newspaper, but on a Sunday in Rhode Island there's not that much to do. I don't believe, especially in a Sunday paper, that people won't stick with a story because there are so many other demands on their time. The story takes its own length and people will stay with it.

You must work hard to find exactly the right ending for your stories.

Yes. I'm looking for it all the time. You know what you need. It's like some kind of a basket where you've got to have a handle on both ends. I want the finish of the story to hold up the weight of the beginning. I want the whole thing balanced. You have to trust the editors for this. Because some editors I know would chop the last third if they needed a shorter story, and you've lost your best lines.

The ending of your nuclear story—with its reference to the birth of the child—reverberates for me. It's almost symbolic.

The whole story is about children. The nuclear story is about the future. This couple in the story is retired. They are not really concerned for themselves because they feel their lives have pretty much run their course. They are worried—and I think its the heart of the nuclear story—about the future. What's coming? What's going to happen? Are we doing something to the future generation? So the ending about the baby seemed natural. It wasn't meant to be theatrical.

You try to set scenes with your leads. Is that typical with you?

It seemed to be a pattern that I fell into with these particular stories. These were all narrative stories and a sense of place is very important in narrative, to establish the feeling of the people for the land. In each place the land is threatened.

There are theories that relate newswriting to the storytelling tradition of myth and folklore. Aren't you writing versions of the "Plague on the Land" story?

It's sitting around the campfire. It's in the epic tradition. And it's part of newstelling. There are essentially very few stories in fiction or in journalism. We're telling them over and over again. We're telling the story of life fighting death. But you're telling them through the lives of different people. That storytelling tradition is very much in my background. My mother is a Finn and I know the Finnish epics. My grandmother was Mohawk, so I know the old Indian stories as well.

Are you as good a writer today as you were 10 years ago?

I feel as if I'm getting better all the time. I look over my clips from years ago and I feel very strongly that my writing is getting better. I don't want to be one of those deadwood people. I remember them from when I was 20. If I don't feel younger than half the people in this room, I'm going to get myself another job. People talk about older reporters getting stale. I can't afford to get stale. I've got a couple of kids, who've been the inspiration for half the stuff I've done. I've got to support them. So I just work harder, and the stories get better.

How have you dealt with the profession's heightened sensitivity to sexist language in our culture?

I am a feminist. I lead a feminist life. But I get very bored with the cliches of contemporary feminism. I'm very quick to yell tripe. I use what seems most graceful, and yes, I'm very aware of it. I will work hard to avoid problems. But finally I use what to my ear is most graceful.

Why aren't you an editor?

I hate being an editor. I've tried it from time to time. If I were an editor I'd probably have more prestige and get invited to niftier places. But I'm a writer. I do that better than anything else.

Photo by Sigrid Estrada

Ellen Goodman

1980 Prize Winner

Commentary

COMMENTS

Faithful readers of Ellen Goodman know a good deal about her: that she's still tall for her age, grows vegetables but has trouble with zucchini, has a terrific daughter, conks out at dinner parties but rises early and cheerfully.

We also know a good deal about her vision of the world, for more than any commentator, Goodman is able to link our public and private histories.

"The most vital concerns can't be divided into internal and external affairs," she writes in her introduction to *Close to Home*, a collection of her columns. "What is more private a concern than the public policy decision made about the family? What is more public a concern than the impact of divorce, or the new isolation, or the two-worker family. The ups and downs of presidential polls are no more crucial to our society than the way we raise our children."

After graduating from Radcliffe College in 1963, Ellen Goodman worked as a reporter and researcher for *Newsweek,* went on to the *Detroit Free Press* and, since 1967, has written for the *Boston Globe.*

In 1973 she received a Nieman Fellowship and studied the dynamics of social change in America, returning to *The Globe* as a columnist. Her interest in the changing roles of men and women led to the book *Turning Points* in 1979.

She writes two columns a week, 750 words each, rain or shine, and subscribes to the notion "that writing a column is like being married to a nymphomaniac: every time you think you're through, you have to start all over again."

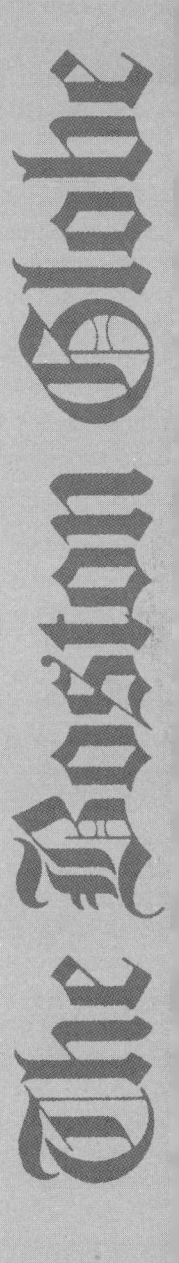

Goodman writes about people, politics, families, sex, foibles and herself. Her work, syndicated through the Washington Post Writers Group, now appears in more than 200 papers.

When Ellen Goodman writes, people read. Whether she's writing about savings accounts or sperm banks, she enlivens her prose with riveting insights, telling understatements, amusing overstatements and apt allusions. The allusions, like her interests, range from Carly Simon to St. Paul.

The five columns reprinted here illustrate her depth and versatility.

There is a nostalgic, but unsentimental piece on our collective sense of loss 16 years after the death of John Kennedy. The occasion for the reflection is the dedication of the Kennedy library, and she begins with the narrative style that is her trademark: "At the very end, Jack Kennedy's voice sailed out over the stillness of the landscape around the library and left a wake of goosebumps across the surface of the crowd. For a few minutes politics was replaced by a profound and silent sense of loss."

Her tightly constructed, almost seamless prose carries us from the recorded voice of JFK back to a time of national idealism, when a 22-year-old Ellen Goodman was beginning her career, through the traumatic years of Vietnam and Watergate, to our contemporary political confusion. The thoughtful essay asks more questions than it answers, a virtue not a flaw, and provokes us to ask our own personal questions about the life and death of JFK.

With a strong background in history, Goodman often creates in her columns a historical context for understanding contemporary events. We see the problems of modern adolescence with greater sensitivity after Goodman has traced, however briefly, the role of children in nineteenth and early twentieth century societies. The notorious Rideout case, involving the question of rape within marriage, becomes more understandable in the light of legal precedents that treated wives as the property of husbands.

But even her most serious subjects are flavored with the pervasive Goodman wit: "Historically, wives, were regarded as property. Once a man bought his own acre, he was allowed to plow it, fence it in, and generally do with it what he would."

That wit stands center stage in a typical bit of self-revelation, Goodman's confession that she dozes off at dinner parties: "It is a rite of passage to be able to debate SALT at midnight. But the only thing that interests me about Brezhnev at that hour is the 'z', or the 'zzzzz.'"

An interview with Ellen Goodman brings the good-humored wisdom of her columns to life. She is tall, blond, and looks a decade younger than her 39 years. She has a lively, expressive face and a crazy voice that tinge her opinions with irony.

If she has a weakness as a writer, it is that she often misses the opportunity to use dialogue creatively, as in her piece on the narcoleptic effects of dinner parties.

But she is becoming, in all other respects, one of the most important writers of opinion in America. Her work is a remedy for the disease of humorlessness that infects the nation's editorial pages. At its best, Ellen Goodman's work is both nourishing and funny, chicken soup with chicken feathers on the side.

Four days after receiving the ASNE Writing Award, she was awarded the Pulitzer Prize for commentary.

JANUARY 2, 1979

Once upon a time there was a charming judge named Matthew Hale who made a certain reputation for himself in seventeenth century England for the ardor with which he ordered the hanging of witches.

This fellow Hale was also one of the earliest recorded advocates of "spousal exclusion," the notion that husbands couldn't, by definition, "rape" their wives because, as he put it so charmingly, "the wife hath given up herself in this kind unto the husband which she cannot retract."

Well, lest you burn Hale's effigy at the stake, remember that in those days husbands were also encouraged to "discipline" their wives. As Blackstone recorded in the eighteenth century, "the law thought it reasonable to entrust him with this power of restraining her by domestic chastisement. . ."

Historically, wives were regarded as property. Once a man bought his own acre, he was allowed to plow it, fence it in, and generally do with it what he would.

The primary function of the law was to protect the "property owner" from any interference or trespassing.

Well, after centuries of rule by this English Common Law, during which sex was coyly referred to as "exercising marital rights," there has finally been pressure for what might be called new zoning laws.

The law is now more concerned with protecting the individual from violence, even domestic violence — such as child abuse and wife battering. Moreover in four states marriage is no longer a defense against the accusation of rape.

The rape laws were reformed in order to protect women from random sexual attacks by their estranged husbands and they have been used effectively this way.

But last week in Oregon, for the first time, a woman named Greta Rideout accused her husband John of rape while they were living together as husband and wife.

The jury of eight women and four men was faced with some extraordinary questions. The members were asked to determine the essence of the Rideouts' private relationship — the marital context in which this act took place. They were asked to decide the difference between what the defense described as a neurotic relationship and what the prosecution described as criminal behavior.

They were not asked to determine, constitutionally, whether a husband should be immune from rape charges, but rather whether this particular man would be found guilty, convicted and jailed for up to 20 years as a rapist.

Full of what I think were reasonable doubts, they found John Rideout not guilty of first-degree rape.

But, I don't believe that this ruling is a renewed license for every husband who wants to "exercise his marital rights" as if his wife had no more say than a gym mat. Nor do I believe as Greta Rideout said that this is a "terrible, terrible setback for women."

I suspect that we will go on striking spousal exclusion clauses from rape law because they are a holdover from the mindset of the days when judges hanged witches and men married property. And we will go on using these laws carefully, sparingly.

It is far more appropriate, accurate and practical to deal with the issues of sexual assault — in or out of marriage — as a crime of violence rather than a crime of sex.

The cry of "rape," especially in marriage, is too loaded an accusation to be very useful. It's not enough to say, as the sign in the women's center in Salem, Oregon did, that "when a woman says no, it's rape." That's a fine piece of consciousness-raising but not a good piece of law enforcement.

Every psychological profile shows that the rapist is out to harm women, not to "have a good time." The husband who forces sex upon his wife is more interested in punishment and power than in pleasure.

It was violence which, according to both Rideouts, preceded their sexual encounter. Forced sex should be dealt with like any other assault, according to the degree of physical and emotional pain inflicted on the victim.

The issue after all is to protect people from harm. Forced sex is to normal intercourse as battering is to caressing.

Changing the accusations from "rape" to assault might not make these decisions easier for a jury. But I think they would clarify the issues — removing from our minds layers of sexual fantasies and historical "rights."

Forcing sex is not, after all, making love. It's making war.

MARCH 6, 1979

"When I was a child, I spake as a child, I understood as a child, I thought as a child. But when I became a man, I put away childish things."
Corinthians I

What about the years in between childhood and adulthood? How do we speak then? How do we think? How do we become men and women?

For most of history there was no in-between, no adolescence as we know it. There was no such lengthy period of semi-autonomy, economic "uselessness," when the only occupation of a son or daughter was learning.

In the eighteenth century, Americans weren't legally adults until they turned 21, but they did important work on farms by seven or eight. When they were physically grown, at only 13 or 16, they had virtually the same jobs as any other adult.

In those days, education was irregular at best, but each child had his or her own vocational guidance teacher: the family. So the transition to adulthood was handled — though not always easily or without tension — through a long apprenticeship, on the farm or in a craft, by people who could point out a direct social path to adulthood.

It was industrialization that changed all that. In the nineteenth century, mills and factories replaced farms, and cities replaced the countryside. Children didn't automatically follow their parents' occupations and so family relations became less important for job training than something called school.

In that century, the need for child labor on farms diminished and the horrors of industrial child labor became widespread. So we passed laws against child labor and in favor of mandatory education. Decade by decade we have raised both ages.

School has replaced work not just out of our benevolence. There are also deep economic reasons. In 1933, at the height of the depression, the National Child Labor Committee put it as baldly as this: "It is now generally accepted that the exploitation of children, indefensible on humanitarian grounds, has become a genuine economic menace. Children should be in school and adults should have whatever worthwhile jobs there are."

School became the place of reading and writing and certification. It provided the necessary paper for employment. School not only kept young people out of the marketplace but promised "better" jobs if they stayed and studied.

The result of all this is clear: today, school is what young people do for a living.

In 1870, less than five percent of the high school age group were in high school. In 1976, 86.1 percent of those 14 to 17 were in school. In 1977, nearly one-third of the 18 to 21-year-olds were in college.

There has been a 129 percent increase in college enrollment in this country since 1960. In many places today, community colleges are entered as routinely as high schools.

While a high school diploma or a college degree no longer guarantees a job, there are more and more jobs you can't even apply for without them. So the payoff is less certain, but the pressure is even greater to go to school longer and longer, to extend the state of semi-autonomy further and further.

The irony is that society worries more when the young try to grasp at adult "privileges" than when they remain in the passive fraternity-house state of mind. We worry about teenage drinking and driving and pregnancy — all perhaps misguided attempts at "grown-up behavior" yet we offer few alternatives, few meaningful opportunities for adulthood training. We have virtually allowed sex, drinking and driving to become rites of passage.

School just isn't enough. It demands only one skill, tests only one kind of performance. From a premed dorm to an Animal House, it is a youth ghetto where adults are only authority figures, where students don't get the chance to test their own identities, their own authority, their own responsibility to others.

Without enough alternatives, we have left schools the job of producing adults. But schools are where the young are kept, not where they grow up.

Adolescence isn't a training ground for adulthood now. It is a holding pattern for aging youth.

JUNE 28, 1979

Let me begin in self-defense by saying that I have never put a lamp shade on my head, or ended an evening pleading for another chorus of "Melancholy Baby."

That, as they say, is the good news.

But the fact of the matter is that I have a social flaw forgiven only among octogenarians and people suffering jet lag. I fall asleep at dinner parties.

I always have. When I was eight and at a restaurant, my parents would order dinner and two chairs: one for my head and one for my feet. When I was 17, I was the only one at the senior prom who went into deep REM instead of high gear during the all-night feast.

If the size of my slippers hadn't eliminated any possibility of being cast as Cinderella, the state of my eyelids would have. I never could have stayed at the ball until midnight.

I come by this trait honorably. After years of politics, my father developed catnapping into a fine art. He could fall asleep in the living room — anyone's living room — and wake up 10 minutes later insisting that he had just been "resting his eyes." He always managed to look at this, like everything else, positively. He assured me that falling asleep was a symptom of being profoundly relaxed and self-assured.

But virtually everyone else I know considers it a problem. It seems that those of us who follow our internal bedtimes alienate more hosts and hostesses than if we had whistled "Dixie" while chewing saltines over their shag rugs.

They do not think: Isn't it wonderful that she is so comfy in our home! They think: what a creep! They are insulted. In fact, they generally regard a mummy on the sofa with a hostility otherwise reserved for the Early Exiter. Both are taken as proof of a dull evening.

Because of this, we are all required by the rules of modern etiquette to (1) stay late and (2) stay up. I can do one or the other.

Obviously, I am unfit for the wonderful world of grown-ups. A world in which hosts invite guests to dinner at 7:30, expect them at 8:30, feed them at 9:30 and begin ardent discussions with them at 11:30.

Hopelessly gauche, I arrive at 7:30, am famished by 8:30, desperate by 9:30 and asleep by 11:30.

It is a rite of passage to be able to debate SALT at midnight. But the only thing that interests me about Brezhnev at that hour is the 'z', or the 'zzzzz.'

But people do not invite you over to sleep with them, at least not in the literal sense. The only one I know who completely sympathizes with my plight is the husband of one of my best friends who suffers from the same antisocial disease. We have, in fact, often and publicly slept together. Neither of us took it personally.

I wish I could say that this habit was related to late-night feedings, because the parents of infants are excused for dozing wherever they can. They have a note from the pediatrician. But the only midnight snacks my daughter has these days are taken with friends, cousins and other army ants at what is called a sleepover. (A sleepover is an eat-over with as little sleep as possible.)

Still, I think that those of us who fade early and often are not bored, rude or miserable. It's just that we live on our own daylight savings time. We go through life as if everyone else were in California and we just arrived from the East Coast.

We are a much maligned and guilt-ridden minority which sleeps to the beat of a different pendulum.

After all, people are not considered antisocial if they refuse to speak before 10 a.m. We do not shun friends because they doze at dawn and are incoherent at breakfast. Being cranky before coffee is considered sophisticated, adult.

Yet, most of us who sleep after dinner are utterly scintillating over orange juice. We are astute with our eggs. We peak at about 9 a.m. And are made to feel guilty, rather overbearing, for that, too.

I think it is high time that we stopped feeling responsible for the droop of our eyelids. Am I my eyelids' keeper? I intend to hold an elegant breakfast party, promptly at six in the morning. Anyone who is unable to discuss nuclear energy over cantaloupe will be cast asunder.

AUGUST 28, 1979

Once, when I studied history for a non-living, I became fascinated with emigrants. For a time I read everything I could find about the people who left for America, about their profound disruption, their strengths, their heroism.

Perhaps it was my prejudice as an American, but in those days I thought very little about the people who stayed behind.

But lately I've been wondering about the difference between those who emigrated and those who didn't. I wonder whether one person remained in Ireland or Italy or Russia because he was content or because he was resigned. I wonder whether another left because she was desperate or because she was hopeful. Was one person more adventurous or another more committed?

In the most desperate moments — the potato famines, the pogroms — which took the greater strength of character: endurance or uprooting? Who were the heroes and who were the martyrs? The emigrants or those who remained behind?

I am thinking about this, I'm sure because many of my friends are turning 40. It began happening three years ago and will, at this rate, continue for at least another five.

Forty is, I observe from not too great a distance, an awkward age. It's an age at which people have histories and options. At 30, they had perhaps less history. At 50, perhaps fewer options.

But at 40, it hangs in the balance. The status quo is weighed against the possible. The person we thought we might be still challenges the person we are. At 40, many reassess themselves and their circumstances. They try to come to terms with their limits or break out of them.

I don't want to force the emigrant analogy. For many of our ancestors, the only option was survival and the only feeling was despair. But for a people who now contemplate leaving lives the way their forebearers left homelands, the comparison is fair enough.

I think we have as much difficulty knowing what is right or wrong, what is brave or foolish, destructive or adventurous, resigned or realistic when we look at our modern lives.

I know, for example, a writer who turned 40 and decided that he was, after all, only a minor talent. He would never be Will Shakespeare, he said, and settled down to a job writing advertising copy. Was he a quitter or a realist? Did he sell himself short or did he find his place?

I know a woman who turned 40 and decided after years of marital indecision and separation that this was her husband, her life — this was "it." It was, she said, okay. Did she settle for less or did she settle down?

On the other hand, there is the 40-year-old man who decided that his history was rot and, to change his future, he left much of the past. How does one judge his action? By just how intolerable his circumstances were? By what his future brings? Did it take more guts to leave than to stay?

My mind curves around all these things like a question mark. It is hard to hold still long enough to make sense of them. I wonder again if we can only judge actions by motivations. Is the person who endures masochistic or virtuous? Is the person who takes off sane or irresponsible?

Introspection is as painful as it is inevitable. At some time in our lives, especially, our mid-lives, we take stock like a department store. We face our selves and our circumstances. We try to be reasonable about our lives, compare what we have (and could lose) with what we might have. We talk about the necessity of compromising and the fear of compromising ourselves. Our satisfactions battle our fantasies.

We try to make rational judgments, I suppose, about protecting the status quo or changing it. But in the end, some of us emigrate to our new worlds and some of us stay with the familiar. And the future historians will have trouble understanding the differences.

OCTOBER 25, 1979

At the very end, Jack Kennedy's voice sailed out over the stillness of the landscape around the library and left a wake of goosebumps across the surface of the crowd. For a few minutes politics was replaced by a profound and silent sense of loss.

The symptoms were as familiar and predictable as the lump in the throat, the hand at the mouth, the tears. But all weekend, after many of the Kennedy people had gone home and the city was basking in Indian summer, I kept wondering about that loss.

What is it that Jack Kennedy's words invariably tap in so many of us? What button is pushed by the sound of his voice? Is it a sense of loss for the man, or for a time in our lives, or for a time in our country's life?

I was in college when Kennedy was President. I was 22 years old and three months into my first job when he was killed. Although I was as realistic as most of those whose family business is politics, my own youthful sense of possibilities coincided with Kennedy's call to get the country moving again.

Now, according to all the actuarial tables, I am in the middle. Those of my generation have lived through 16 years of public life that sounded alarm bells across the text books: Vietnam, Watergate, the energy crisis, inflation. Also we have lived through 16 years of private life in which most of us have made the major decisions about work, children.

Today, like many of my generation, I sense that my choices no longer range from A to Z, but perhaps from A to E. This is not a complaint, just an observation.

In mid-life most of us feel these limits. We don't squander our energy; we allot it with care. We call this maturing. The young call it aging.

But when I hear his voice, his words, I feel a loss. Is it loss for a time and attitude of life which I have outgrown as irrevocably as I have outgrown naivete? Or is it loss for a time of his country's life, before lowering our expectations became our best protection from disappointment?

I have heard friends wonder about this in other contexts. It is not merely a question about our past and present. It may very well determine the future — whether a "call to battle" rouses us or repels us as a foolish children's crusade.

Are we just playing possum, as Carly Simon sang, or have we really changed?

Before Jimmy Carter left Boston, he said that he and Ted Kennedy differed on little, only spending and arms. But I heard other differences on the platform that day, different approaches to our psychology.

Carter talked about living in a time of "limits" and an age of "hard choices." He said that, "We are struggling with a profound transition from a time of abundance to a time of growing scarcity in energy."

Ted Kennedy for his part talked about challenges that are opportunities, and spirits that "soar." About Jack he said, "He understood that America is at its best when the nation is on the move, when ideas are on the march.... He filled America with pride and made this nation young again."

Both were, of course, delivering their own Saturday sermon versions of the Jack Kennedy text. But they may have opened a dialogue that is really familiar to those of us in mid-life — between limits and opportunities, fiscal realities and challenges, hard choices and historical purpose.

Before the opening of the library, a cast of Jack Kennedy's people had spread out through the city talking to high school students. Historian Arthur Schlesinger put this argument another way at my former high school. He said, "I do not see American political history in terms of liberal versus conservative, but rather in terms of exhaustion versus vitality."

Clearly he associated Jack Kennedy with vitality, Carter with exhaustion and Ted Kennedy with renewed vitality. The senator echoed that in Philadelphia Oct. 22 when he said Americans want "actions, not excuses." But those of us who were young with Jack may not see it quite that simply.

Whether we back Kennedy or Carter may depend on whether we see our own political history as an energy cycle or as a progression. It may depend on whether we regard "limits" as a phrase of mid-life depression — an excuse for defeat — or of mature realism. Whether we see Carter's "hard choices" as "excuses" or facts. Whether we see, "opportunities" as renewed hope or youthful delusions.

In short, it may depend on what we were mourning when we heard Jack Kennedy's words on the Boston shore.

LMN

CONVERSATIONS

CLARK: In one of the columns in your book, you say that you put a bit of information into a file labeled "Fathers." Do you have a complicated filing system?

GOODMAN: I don't want to come across as a paragon of organization, because that would be so far beyond the truth. But I do clip. We all clip. I strive to make various files of things that I might read from time to time. And I'm more or less successful depending on the astrology. None of us have any clerical help. So I have a very haphazard mental and physical filing system.

How do you get your ideas for columns?

You don't really know you're collecting ideas for columns, but things sit in the back of your head. Today, for example, I'm doing a column involved in the "psychiatrization" of the country: psychiatrists turning social problems into emotional problems. What pushed my button was something in the paper. It was all the Three Mile Island shrinks running around. But what I had in the back of my head for some time was an incident on a DC10. A flight attendant told me that any flight attendant who doesn't want to fly these things is sent to a shrink. Several things were floating around. Psychiatrists came out and said it was the media's fault that everybody was worried about nuclear energy. They're not doing anything at Three Mile Island except have a $375,000 National Institute of Mental Health grant to see how people live with stress. Where if I had $375,000 I'd take all those people and get them the hell out of there. But the government is dealing with their emotional problems. The thing in my business is making the links.

When you clip out something where does it go?

It goes on the top of my desk. Did you see my desk? (She points to a small slushpile of papers and clippings.) It also goes in something that I've had ever since I worked at *Newsweek,* which is a futures file. And I also have a little list in my confuser—my Freudian slip—my computer of story ideas.

How does an idea translate into a column?

Often in our business you're working out of desperation, ya know, the most important thing looming ahead of you is the deadline. I'm responsible for two columns a week—750 words each. I have the same number of words whether I'm dealing with China or with your shoelaces. So some weeks I have a lot of ideas. But some weeks... nnnnnnnnnnrrrrrrr... the brain wave is totally flat. Everybody strives to keep a sort of average. You hope that your worst is a C plus. You're going for the long run. You can't expect to hit an A all the time. But you have to get enough professionalism that you're rarely going below B minus or C plus.

What are the problems involved in only getting to devote 750 words to, say, a Kennedy retrospective or a piece on your sleeping at dinner parties?

The biggest problem to me is that most of your reporting ends up on the cutting room floor. When I'm doing something that requires a lot of research, my draft may be 109 lines, and then I've got to get back on the outside to 82. And usually I'm hitting 75. And if I don't do it, the *Chicago Sun-Times* is gonna do it. I'll be in an airport, I'm gonna pick up a paper and see that somebody else has cut it. So I've got to edit myself pretty carefully. If I spend three days reporting a piece, I've got to get rid of 80 percent of the stuff, because after all it's an opinion piece. You've got to concentrate on style, on ideas. You've got time for one idea, and the columns that I feel don't work are when I'm trying two ideas.

Give me an example of one that didn't work.

The column in this morning's paper. Half the column was a correction and half the column was about Reagan. I wanted to get that correction in, and I think I ruined what could have been a very interesting column on Reagan.

The columns in your book "Close to Home" are divided into different categories: our times, people, women, personals, relationships, family, parents and children, foibles, social issues. Do you think of these categories when you write?

I'm very conscious of range. You don't want to become a one-note Charlie. I have several areas of interest, which change, because after all I'm writing for a newspaper, so I'm constantly responding to the news. Four years ago I wasn't writing on Bio-ethics because there wasn't anything going on that we knew about. The subjects change as the times change.

Are there things you don't write about?

I don't write about foreign policy because I don't know anything about foreign policy. That's my major no-no. I might write off of it if something strikes me as relating to us. But I think there are an awful lot of people in journalism writing about Afghanistan on Monday and Iran on Tuesday and South America on Wednesday and I don't trust them because I know what you can't know.

Do you consciously try to change subjects for your column?

It's also subconscious. I tend to look forward to the time when there's nothing going on in the newspapers so I can write something more of an essay. That's what's different about my column. Other people panic when nothing is going on. I'm relieved. It gives me a chance to play with writing.

I notice in your column on rape and marriage that your news link—the Rideout case—is quite

low. Isn't that risky? Shouldn't the point be higher up?

My links are often fairly far down in the story. That one is lower than usual. Sometimes you consciously get the link way down, because nobody's gonna read it if you get it up high. You don't have to trick people into reading, but you lead people into the story by a narrative. Because if you tell them at the beginning that you're going to be talking about the socio-economic policies of Lower Slobovia, they're going to go ho-hum on you.

Is the 750 word limit a help or a hindrance?

When I was doing feature stories it used to be a joke that one of my editors would pick up something I did and say "Jesus Christ, I'm not going to edit this, I'm going to weigh it." And I would try to write the piece so they couldn't cut it. Even though the piece was long, my transitions were as tight as a drum. That was the skill I developed over 10 years. Then suddenly I had to edit myself. Well this machine helps me because you know what line you're on all the time. You know when to start worrying.

I've occasionally heard your work criticized as superficial. Is superficiality the columnist's plight?

To a certain extent. I think its also a function of trying to see significance in the things you're talking about. Sometimes if you had the time and a few more links it would work better. And sometimes, like everybody else, my thought processes are superficial. One of the nice things about writing a column is that if you've done a bad one—and I'm my toughest grader—you can go back later and do it again on the same topic. I can think of lots of times when I've covered two percent of the topic.

So you accept the fact that you may not be able to get too deeply into your subject?

You're writing for a newspaper. And maybe your friends and my friends want things at a sophisticated, deep level. But you're writing for a newspaper. You're not writing for the *New York Review of Books*. You've got to take people where they are. You can't do a Jerry Brown on them. You know. (She deepens her voice and does a Jerry Brown imitation.) "This is where I am, and if you happen to understand me. . ." No. You have to explain your thought process, lay out the way you think through these things, so they will follow you and think you are reasonable. I've been criticized for using big words. Well I have a big vocabulary. But I'm trying for a balance. You try not to write beyond people so they don't understand you, yet you try not to insult them. Particularly when you're dealing with women's issues because the levels of understanding are exceptionally low.

Do you write to please yourself or your readers?

I'm conscious that I'm writing to persuade others. Some of my writing involves my own thought processes, thinking myself through the issue. I don't know if you've read that statement by Alfred Kazin: "I write for myself and others. The others, dear reader, are an afterthought." Well, that's not quite true in journalism. But in terms of style, rhythms, I'm writing to satisfy my own ear.

Columnists are criticized for "instant analysis." Do you ever feel that you'd like to mull things over a while before rushing to an opinion?

I have two feelings about that. I've been in journalism my whole adulthood, since I was 22, and I'm very oriented to write it and get it in the paper. That's the name of the game. Most of the stuff we write isn't going to be put in the capsule for the year 2000. But relative to newspapers, I can sit back, I have time and perspective. Newspapers serve two functions. They tell you what's going on. And they tell you what it means. So the columnist is important to a public which is inundated with facts. I am, relative to most journalists, sitting back, expressing what it means. But I am not writing a scholarly treatise. And yes, there are times when I would like to sit back and write a much longer piece. Those times basically I write a book, or a magazine piece.

You have a background in history, and I notice in a couple of these pieces you try to establish a historical context for understanding contemporary events.

Last week I wrote on the eugenicists. The reason I do write from some kind of perspective is that most of us have the historical perspective of a mushroom. We keep inventing the wheel, we keep making policy statements as if nobody ever tried it before. It seems to me so destructive. At the very least people ought to know that eugenicists existed before what's-his-name and his sperm bank.

How do you get the background material. How did you find Matthew Hale, for example.

I have a lot of books on various and sundry topics that I'm interested in. And I also have people who I call, who will help me out. In family law and children's law there are a couple of people I count on. Also in history and biology.

You write about yourself a lot. Is that the real Ellen Goodman, or is it a persona that is useful for the column.

There are parts of yourself that you are willing to share and parts that you are not. I don't write confessional journalism. And although there are people who do that well, most people who write confessional journalism have got five columns in them. Its important to me to express the range of things that people are interested in. The way we really live. I have a job. But I also have a child. I also have a vegetable garden. We have to establish credibility because the public doesn't believe us. One way to do that is to say

"You know I'm a person going through the world, and you know I get depressed, my friends turn 40 and get divorced, my zucchini won't grow. . . ." There's nothing I have written which is false about myself. But there are many things I don't care to share.

When I read Nora Ephron, I feel I know a lot of personal things about her.

On the other hand, you know nothing about George Will, Scotty Reston, Tom Wicker. Nothing. I'm not interested in either of those positions.

Why do you write so much from your own experience?

You write from who you are. What I don't like as a reader is when someone is telling me the Truth. What is the Truth? When I write I say "Now let me give you a few of my prejudices, my points of view, and now let me tell you what I think about this issue. You follow me. You agree with me if you want to. And respect me if you don't. It's up to you. But I'm giving you enough information so that you can judge.

I notice that you constantly make links between personal history and the history of our times.

That's probably my own neurosis more than a plot. I do have the urge, this is in perfectly Eriksonian terms, to encompass rather than to separate out. I'm interested in seeing the links. I mean I'll do that in conversation. There has been much too much separation in journalism. Anything "personal" went on the women's pages; anything "serious" went into the newshole. So such "unserious" topics as what you eat, and who you marry, and how you raise your children, are put in the women's pages and the "serious" things such as the latest straw poll from Iowa were put in the newshole. Well who's making those decisions. I want to break down those barriers between what's private and what's public that are part of the general social insanity. So while you say that its exceptional for me to see the links, I think its extraordinary that it isn't routine.

You have a wonderful sense of humor, and you communicate it skillfully in print.

Sometimes. It's the thing that everybody is most insecure about. Humorous columns. I never know if they're funny till somebody else has read them. I came from a family in which humor was the main defusing activity. My father was a very funny man. He was in politics and often went for the joke and lost the vote. I like Russell Baker's eccentric humor. I like slightly off the wall, highly exaggerated humor. I will forgive people a lot if they are funny. I think it's very underrated as a thing that gets you through life. But in journalism? Well I judged a national magazine awards last week and I was horrified that there was no humor. No humor! Nothing funny! What's going on?

There's very little dialogue in your writing, am I right about that?

Yes. It's funny because my daughter who writes very well—I think she's going to be a playwright or something—because she writes all dialogue. She writes these long stories that are almost all dialogue, and I've thought about it, after reading my stuff—that I don't.

Do you think about sentence length, rhythm, paragraph length?

Take out a sentence and make it into a paragraph. Visual things. I use a lot of capital letters. The attempt to make it oral, to make your points physically. You're so limited that you've got to work with whatever you can. For a time I used a lot of sounds. Urrrggghh! I don't do that so much any more.

Do you rewrite much?

Auuuggghh! I rewrite constantly. I almost finished my first draft before lunch. I'll spend hours rewriting. Actually that's the fun. I spend the afternoon polishing it.

Do you still consider yourself a reporter?

There are lots of ways in which you report. The first is by going through the world. You report when you go with your daughter to class. You report when you go to the supermarket. And some of it is reporting in the classic sense. I spend a lot of time on the phone. To have an opinion you have to do all the reporting you would on the story. Plus you've got to figure out what to think. What's the old Pete Hamill line: "It's the hardest job in the world that doesn't involve heavy lifting."

How do you deal with the problem of sexist language?

I don't have any problem at all. I'd like to say on the record that people who find it a problem enjoy focusing in on it as if it were a great difficulty of modern society. It's a lot of bull. I rarely use *he* as a generic, and I almost never have a problem with it. Use a plural. Use *he* and *she*. There are 42 ways to write around it. There are things I don't use or like. I avoid titles when possible. I don't like *chairperson*. *Chair* is fine. I find it shocking that *The New York Times* still refers to the founder of *Ms. Magazine* as Miss Steinem. It's incorrect. When they reviewed my book, they referred to me as Miss Ellen Goodman. One, Goodman is my married name. Two, I'm divorced. It's so inaccurate that you have to come to the conclusion that they would rather be punitive than accurate. They can call me Goodman. They can call me Goodperson!

1980 FINALISTS

Dudley Clendinen
Pete Dexter
Richard Ben Cramer
Francis X. Clines
Michael Daly
Mark Bowden
Bill Lyon
W.D. (Zeke) Wigglesworth
Barry Bearak
Martin Bernheimer
Paul Galloway

CHICAGO Sun-Times
The Philadelphia Inquirer
York Times
DAILY NEWS
Newspaper
THE MINNEAPOLIS STAR
Copyright 1980 Minneapolis Star and Tribune Company
Times
The New York Times
Los Angeles Times
PHILADELPHIA DAILY NEWS
The People Paper
The News American
St. Petersburg Times
Los Angeles
DAILY
The Philadelphia Inquirer
THE PHILADELPHIA DAILY NEWS
NEWS
The Miami Herald
CHICAGO Sun-Times
THE BRIGHT ONE
DAILY NEWS
DAILY NEWS
America's Largest Newspaper
The Miami Her

DUDLEY CLENDINEN

St. Petersburg Times

Dudley Clendinen wrote for the St. Petersburg Times *for 11 years before joining* The New York Times *early in 1980. This piece is the first of a series that resulted in a special state investigation of vote-buying in northern Florida.*

FEBRUARY 25, 1979

ROCK BLUFF — A cold, misting rain drifted through the pine woods. Dusk. Almost dark. A dimming, filtered gray light, and in the middle of it, a clearing at the bend of a U-shaped cut of yellow rutted road, the paintless gray clapboard shack of Kinzie Atkins. No sign of life. No car in front. No light coming from the house.

But oddly, the portentous, booming, upbeat voice of a sportscaster. It issued in puffs of sound through the thin wood walls and ebbed and welled across the clearing through the lonesome rain. "Willie Mays," the voice said. And "Willie Mays" again.

Willie Mays, a black man, age 45, had made the Baseball Hall of Fame.

And Kinzie Atkins, a black man, age 45, who was born here and is still here and will die here, leaned back in silence on the cool torn vinyl of the couch in the dark, unfinished shell of a house in the misting woods and listened to the news of the induction of Willie Mays.

The Hall of Fame. How 'bout that? And Kinzie Atkins smiled.

Then we knocked on the door. He turned on a light and let us in.

Kinzie Atkins is a large, pot-bellied, smiling man, very genial on the outside. Maybe he smiles because he didn't expect life to be any more than it is, or maybe he did and smiles to fill in the empty places. At any rate, he has a face wreathed in jolly creases, and a clouded, doubtful gaze. Kinzie has glaucoma and is legally blind, has been for a long time. Two of his brothers, Judge and Eddie, are, too.

Kinzie lives alone in the woods in the little house, which he rents for $15 a month. He has a regular monthly income of $189.40, a disability check that he gets from the Social Security Administration. Sometimes, he can get a woman in to cook for and stay with him. But for the most part, he lives alone, with a small tan mutt who stays under the house.

He hasn't done regular work in a long time, but he does odd jobs for Mr. Bert Phillips, a white man, an old friend and in-law of Colonel Faircloth's. Phillips has a gas pump and a little one-room canned goods, cigarettes and beer store up on the paved state road. It is from Phillips that Kinzie rents the house, and from Phillips that he buys some of what he needs. It is to Phillips that Kinzie Atkins' check comes in the mail.

"It come in the box — his mailbox," Kinzie said. "He give it to me, I give it back to him. He cash it and give me the money, and I pay what I owe."

Did Phillips give him a bill each month, to show him what he owed?

"I doan see no bill," said Kinzie. "I juss take his word for it. Thass what I been doin' for the last 20 years." In other words, since before the black population in Liberty County dared to vote.

The best estimate of when the blacks here began to vote is 1964. That is the memory of the black —such as it is — leadership here, which got some workers from the Congress of Racial Equality (CORE) in here to conduct a registration drive 15 years ago. But it is a leadership so fearful, from experience, of economic white reprisal that none of them would let me quote him by name. That is the state of Liberty here.

At any rate, since Kinzie got the vote, he says, Bert Phillips has helped him with his voting, too, either by going into the booth with him at the courthouse or by getting an absentee ballot sent down to the store. With Kinzie, it is not hard to do that, because Kinzie cannot read and can barely print his name.

"At the courthouse," Kinzie said, "Miss Clara Belle (Clara Belle Revell, the supervisor of registration. Her husband was once sheriff. Her nephew is now sheriff. Another nephew is principal of one of the county's three schools. The Revells here do quite well.) okayed it, and he (Phillips) did the markin'."

"At the courthouse, I didn't get nothin'," said Kinzie, with his big sloppy smile. "But at Bert's house, I got $10. This time, I got $20."

By "this time," he means the second primary, the Democratic runoff, last Oct. 5. He did not vote in the general election. It wasn't needed. Out of almost 3,000 voters registered in the whole county, there are only 28 Republicans, so the general election doesn't mean a thing.

Kinzie said it happened this way. He was walking down the road one day after the first primary, when Ann Beckwith, Jack Hardy and Betty Beckwith drove up in a car and stopped beside him. Ann, he says, was driving and Jack Hardy was sitting shotgun and Betty was in the back. And Jack Hardy said something like, "I want you all to vote for my men," and went on to name some names, and to mention the superintendent, Skeet Shuler.

"They had this little ole bitty — what'd you call 'em? — had some little ole somethin' to sign," said Kinzie. A request for an absentee ballot. "He said, 'We got somethin' for you if you do it,' " Kinzie said. "I said, 'No, I don't think I'm going to vote.' "

"I ain't heard no more about it," he said, "till Bert was honking the horn for me to come up there. He blows the horn when he's ready for me to come up there."

It was a Tuesday, about 10 or 11 in the morning, Kinzie thinks, when he heard Bert Phillips honk. Kinzie left his house and started walking up toward Bert Phillips' house and store. "Come on in here," he says Phillips told him. "I want you to vote with this lady here."

The lady was Betty Beckwith, Kinzie said, and Ann Beckwith was there, too, in a car in front. And they had his absentee ballot, which he had not requested or authorized them to get.

"He had done got it," Kinzie said. "He had it there."

(There is, in the supervisor of registration's files at the county seat, in Bristol, a typed request, with the date of Sept. 14, 1978 written in. "Mrs. Revell," it says, "I hereby designate Ann Beckwith to pick up my ballot." The message is marked at the bottom with a large "X," on one side of which is written "His Mark," and on the other side, "Kinzie Atkins." There are two things that make that request for an absentee ballot strange. The first is that Kinzie says he never authorized anyone to get it for him. He wasn't going to be absent from the county that day. And he has sworn an affidavit to that effect. The second is that Kinzie does not sign papers with an "X," "His Mark." He signs them with his name, in big, irregular block print. It is the only thing he can write.)

When he went up to the store, said Kinzie, Bert Phillips did not ask him how he wanted his ballot marked. "He had done tole me he wanted me to vote for Joe Brown, (Tom) Stoutamire and Buddy Potter." The Shuler ticket. "He and them did the fillin' out. Didn't ask me nothin'."

And then, he said, "Ann Beckwith called me to the car and gave me two $10 bills and told me not to go to the polls."

So Kinzie hadn't even signed the ballot — the signature wasn't his?

"No," he said. "Just gave me two $10 bills and said, 'Now, don't you show up at the polls.'"

In the supervisor of registration's file at the Liberty County Courthouse is the voter's certificate that purports to attest to the validity of Kinzie Atkins' ballot. The certificate is to be signed, once the ballot has been marked, by the voter and two witnesses to his signature.

On "Kinzie's" certificate, the reason checked for voting absentee is that "I will not be in the county of my residence during the hours the polls are open for voting on election day."

On the line, marked for the voter's signature is an "X," and beside it is written "Kinzie Atkins."

And the ballot is witnessed by the signatures of "Bert Phillips" and "Betty Beckwith."

And that, according to documents and Kinzie's own account, is how the ballot of a blind, illiterate, dependent black man named Kinzie Atkins was taken from him and cast for him in "The Colonel's Precinct" in the second primary of the last election here. And a lawsuit alleges and evidence indicates that Kinzie Atkins was not alone. Far from it. His nephew and two of his brothers swear they did the same. And the reasons they would have are numerous and plain. They are poor and dependent on the goodwill of the whites around them. Jobs are few and hard to get. They need the money. And they are black. Country, backward, subservient, black.

One more brother, Judge, refused, "because I had been sold one time, and I wasn't going to be sold no more."

Some other blacks, poor but proud, poor but independent in their spirit, refused to sell. Some poor whites refused. But the available evidence is that many people sold their votes, for money, or under pressure, or for the promise of a job, or to escape the threat of losing one. There are many ways of bringing pressure here, and most of them are used. You will hear about all of that, from those involved, as this series continues.

A suit challenging the vote is pending in the local circuit court, and the FBI in Washington is considering a request to investigate. But in Liberty County, the history of vote-buying, of electoral fraud, goes back as far as living memory. The purchase of the absentee ballot seems to be simply the present, highest, state of the art.

PETE DEXTER

Philadelphia Daily News

Pete Dexter, a columnist for the Philadelphia Daily News, *has been writing for newspapers for seven years. He writes about "how people work, how they play." Raised in South Dakota, he has also worked as a bouncer, a bartender, a mailman, a beer truck driver, and a door-to-door salesman.*

OCTOBER 5, 1979

BOSTON — The man had come late to Logan Circle, almost as late as the Pope. Half a million people had come earlier, and they were closer to the altar. And that was all right too.

Sitting on the steps of the platform itself, the distance would have been the same. He knew that.

His legs hurt, and he leaned against a small tree. A woman who was out of breath pulled an overweight 10- or 11-year-old-boy in a direction that might have taken them to a place where the Pope would pass on his way to the Cathedral of SS. Peter and Paul. It was hard to tell with all the people. She had the child by the wrist.

"We waited all morning," she said. "We come out here at 5 o'clock in the morning to see the Holy Father, on the greatest day of our life if we could see him and just please be blessed, and then Ronnie got sick."

The man looked into Ronnie's face, and saw the boy didn't quite understand what his mother had said. He smiled at his mother as she told it, though.

She said, "He got into my purse and ate something that made him sick, and we had to go home and clean him up. You can't see the Holy Father looking like that."

Ronnie shook his head no. He looked down at the front of his fresh shirt and said it. "Noooo."

The mother said Ronnie was not right in the head, and hadn't been since he was born. She said it that way, but it came out softer than that. "He's sensitive," she said. "He knows it when you're talking about it. I was hoping that we might see the Holy Father and be blessed. I thought he might touch him . . ."

The woman looked at the crowd and saw that the chances of that were gone. "Once in a lifetime you might see the Pope," she said.

The man said, "Maybe he'll bless you even if you can't see him."

She said, "When his father died, Ronnie was very young, but he knew something was gone. I told him Daddy had gone to live with Jesus. That's how he knows Jesus, that's who his daddy's with . . ."

The woman's purse was straw and not quite drawn together at the top. Ronnie was looking inside while she talked. He put his hand in and she took it out, absently pried a tube of lipstick out of his fingers.

"This chance will never happen again," she said.

Having lost the lipstick, Ronnie looked down and out too. She gave him a Snickers candy bar and he was smiling again. "What a kidder," she said.

Then someplace a long ways off, people began cheering. The woman stood on her toes, but nobody this far away could see the Pope, or even the Pope's car. Then everybody was cheering. Ronnie stood on his toes too. He put the rest of the candy bar in his mouth and began to clap. He couldn't get his mouth closed. He checked his mother's face to see that it was the right thing.

She was crying — probably for 11 different reasons at the same time — but she was clapping too. And for a long moment they held each other's eyes.

The man didn't want to intrude and began to walk around the outside of the crowd, but before he left the woman said one more thing. Not to him, to Ronnie.

She told him, "This is the best day we will ever see."

And the man thought about that as he walked. He knew what it meant, but he didn't understand it. Everywhere he went people were saying that same thing. There was cheering and whistling and banners and buttons and flags, but the feeling was more serious than that. And kinder than that. And no matter what anybody tells you, it was religious.

And the man would have liked to have been part of it, but that wasn't the way things were.

He could understand the Pope. He knew kindness when he saw it. He knew something about love. But the comfort the Pope could offer the man didn't extend beyond that.

John Paul II was a man elected by other men — some of them kind, some of them not — and when this John Paul II stood on the platform and spoke for God, the man felt a distance that he couldn't measure, even as half a million people seemed to come closer together.

What the man could measure was that he was getting older. He looked at the huge white cross on the platform and knew that every day he was a day closer to finding out.

Either that or dropping into a black hole.

But getting closer never changed the distance. He had almost died once, six years before that in the ocean off Key West, Fla., and even then there had been the distance. Always the distance . . .

He remembered what he'd said to the woman with the retarded son. "Maybe he'll bless you even if you can't see him."

It occurred to the man that his own chances were somehow tied up in that sentence too.

RICHARD BEN CRAMER

The Philadelphia Inquirer

Richard Ben Cramer, foreign correspondent for The Philadelphia Inquirer *won the Pulitzer Prize and ASNE Writing Award in 1979 for his Middle East stories. This brief selection comes from "Portrait of a Family," a novella-length story written after Cramer spent a month living with a West Philadelphia family.*

Myrtle Lane in West Philadelphia, hard by the Penn Central's Main Line tracks, is a street of two-story rowhouses that hunker under summer heat in a sweaty squat.

The house already was hot and airless that morning when Monroe woke and carried the color TV set downstairs to the living room, where it would play for the next 16 hours.

Connie Monroe, his wife, came down moments later and asked him to turn the water on. The main valve into the house is kept shut to prevent the leaky plumbing from further damaging the walls.

Mrs. Monroe made the rounds of the living- and dining-room furniture, collecting the clothes that had been left out to dry. Monroe, in the basement, threw the valve.

All five children were up, by the sound of it. Russell Jr., 3, and Paul, 1½, were running and giggling in the second-floor hall. Andrea, 8, came downstairs, rubbing her eyes under her glasses and asking her mother for cereal. Carla, 15, and Cathy, 13, were waiting upstairs for the water to reach the bathroom.

Cathy . . . graduation . . . dress . . . Cathy . . .

Cathy and her dress were on top of the mountain of his worries as Monroe sipped his coffee and lit his first Kool in the dining room.

Her graduation from the eighth grade at Lamberton School was one day away. One day to get the dress. One day to get $20 . . . .

Monroe called his uncle to ask about using the uncle's Sears charge card to pay for Cathy's dress.

"He said the charge was already up to $800," Monroe said after the call. "He said it would have to wait till next week. But kids, you know . . ." Monroe stared into his coffee. "Cathy wouldn't understand that."

On the big color screen, swiveled now to face the dining table, David Hartman was golly-wowing: a square watermelon in Japan, a man-powered flying machine in Britain, 110-degree temperatures in Palm Springs, Calif. . . .

Monroe, 27, stared without seeing. He was not going to Japan. If he was lucky that day, he was going to another uncle's house to work on cleaning and carpentry, to ask thereafter for $20 or so to pay for a new dress for Cathy.

There was laughter in the house now, children's squeals of delight as little Russ got tickled by an older sister, as Paul stuck his tiny foot into his father's big workboot and called out, "Da! Ssoos!"

Monroe didn't notice for a minute, his thoughts occupied with making it; making it past Cathy's graduation, past the shut-off on the water bill, making it up to the next of Connie's welfare checks, making it through Sunday when the church would need his weekly $10, or into the Fourth of July with enough money, say $20, to take his wife and their five children *somewhere* for *something*; no, this was not the making-it that most Philadelphians contemplate and scheme for.

And if the mornings were easier now — no burning in the stomach walls, none of the eyepain of vodka-bright light, none of the mystifying and reproachful looks from Connie and Carla and Cathy (the others were too young to understand), now that drink did not companion his darkness — did this not leave his nights close and fearful, without release from his evening horrors, that tomorrow would offer nothing for food, that dawn would reveal disaster encamped like a gas-man on the broken doorstep, that, even now, the bell of the ice cream truck (how he hated that steady, cheery bell!) would send his children squalling at him, calling for quarters and finding . . .?

Ding, d-ding-ding. "Come and get it," cried the cheery blond mommy to her freckle-faced brood and the screen of the television was filled with the eye-catching label of her lemonade mix . . . .

"Da! Ssoos!"

"Nothing . . .," Monroe said, from out of nowhere.

"Da!"

"Russell," his wife said from the kitchen, where she was wiping up after Andrea's breakfast cornflakes. "Look at Paul."

"All right, Paul, bring it here." Monroe held out his arms to his son, who had grabbed the boot with both little hands and was teetering across the floor toward the table.

"That kid loves shoes," Monroe said. "He's gonna be a shoe salesman."

Paul, with an air of accomplishment, dropped the shoe at his father's feet. Monroe reached down and swept his son into a battered highchair at the table. With a humorless chuckle, he added: "Better be a shoe manufacturer."

In the living room, Russell Jr. fell against a chair and wailed in pain. Paul discovered himself in his highchair and started screaming: "Da! Get out!" Then the phone rang, and, for the first time in months, Monroe was offered a job referral.

Monroe got off the phone and sat silently in the living room for a moment.

"That was a guy from the unemployment," he said to his wife. "They got a job at a warehouse, but it's only three dollars an hour."

Constance Monroe had learned not to push. Still, expectant, she sat across from her husband, waiting.

"We'll have to report it," Monroe said.

Mrs. Monroe just sat, looking anxious, not wanting to seem too eager.

"Da! Get out! Da!"

There was no answer from the living room.

"At first, we kept asking ourselves how we had made our son do this, what had made him . . ." Several parents whose children were homosexuals were confiding in Phil Donahue. Monroe had unconsciously swiveled the TV set to face the living room as he passed.

"You want me to take it?" he asked.

Connie Monroe paused, looking up at her husband through lowered lashes. "Well, how do you feel about it?"

He said, sharply: "I feel about like you feel about it."

She looked up at him and decided to plunge. "Well, I'd take it," she said.

Monroe looked annoyed, as if his doubts had been confirmed.

"No, I mean for me," Mrs. Monroe said, hurriedly. "I mean, I'd take it . . . if I could . . . for me."

But she didn't mean for her.

"OK," said Monroe and he stood suddenly. Mrs. Monroe got up to iron a clean T-shirt for his interview. She detoured toward the kitchen to release Paul, still screaming, from his confining highchair.

FRANCIS X. CLINES

The New York Times

Francis X. Clines joined The New York Times *as a copy boy in December 1958, wrote a column "About New York" from 1976 - 1979, and is now a reporter in the* Times *Washington Bureau. This is one of his stories on the Pope's visit to America.*

OCTOBER 4, 1979

Shifting in delight from the role of world statesman to that of attentive shepherd, Pope John Paul II bade a warm farewell to New York yesterday by sharing laughter and affection with its citizens. Before departing for Philadelphia, the next stop on his weeklong national tour, the Pope turned a rain-drenched packed house at Shea Stadium into an exuberant parish gathering.

"Above all, a city needs a soul if it is to become a true home for human beings," the Pontiff declared in farewell. "You, the people, must give it this soul."

The crowds during his second day in the city were as much moved by the Pope's gentle asides and salutes to separate groups and neighborhoods as they were by formal exhortations.

New Yorkers waited at the Battery, soaked, near Ellis Island's once-frenzied immigration center, to hear the Pope praise the city's ethnic underpinnings.

In a well-received ecumenical note, the Pope paused in his address near the harbor and declared: "I address a special word of greeting to the leaders of the Jewish community, whose presence here honors me greatly."

Then, speaking as a native of Poland of the abomination of the Auschwitz death camp, he saluted the Jewish community: "Shalom! Peace be with you!"

Even with the morning rain, the Pope seemed a more relaxed man making his closing rounds. He seemed to be recharging his spirit following the exhausting schedule

Tuesday that was built around a detailed human-rights speech at the United Nations.

At Madison Square Garden, the Pope basked in the affection of 19,000 teenagers, accepting their gifts of a T-shirt, jeans, guitar and tape cassette of their music. And when they interrupted his tight schedule with impromptu pep cheers of fondness, he beamed at their exuberance. In response, he offered a mellifluous crooning sound of exclamation — the Polish equivalent of "Wow!" according to one of his fellow countrymen.

In the same spirit, John Paul lingered over the small details of his goodbye at Shea Stadium. He evoked partisan roars as he saluted the parts of the metropolis with slow, deep-voiced care: "Long Island. New Jersey. Connecticut. And Brooklyn."

His pronunciation of the latter — "Broke-leen" — was savored by the crowd, and they responded with their biggest roar of outer-borough, suburbanite approval.

Before the parting was done, sunlight shafted down, and even the Pope paused at this breakthrough in the heavens. By that time the crowd felt close enough to laugh with the Pope over his mispronunciation of the towers of commerce in Manhattan as "skyscrappers."

The teenagers at Madison Square Garden paid the Pope the compliment of shouting some rock-concert salutations: "All-riiight!" Then, as the rounds of papal pep cheers echoed back and forth, John Paul sat merrily and shared their fun.

In a media show on a screen overhead, pictures of local teens, accompanied by taped messages of appreciation and even advice, were offered to the Pontiff.

"I think women wouldn't make bad priests," one girl's voice sounded politely from the screen. It was the first bit of mild audacity on the feminism issue to be heard on the papal tour. It was not clear, however, whether the Pope heard the girl's voice over the canned background music — an upbeat sound, but more in the cola-commercial way than the top-40 way of teenagers.

Reluctantly the Pope took heed of his schedule and, playing the gentle shepherd, he silenced his audience so he could speak. Using his voice like the actor's tool it was in his youth, John Paul offered the teen-agers advice, soft-toned for emphasis: "When you wonder about the mystery of yourself, look to Christ."

The gathering of the youth and the Pope seemed one of the most emotional stops thus far for the 59-year-old church leader. He swept the young crowd with an intense stare, nodding, waving, thanking them in what seemed a religious experience of deep, inarticulate feeling. The teen-agers roared their delight as he carefully studied their gifts, and they serenaded him with the folk songs they now sing at the modernized mass.

Music marked much of the Pope's day. At 7 A.M. a choir on Madison Avenue near 50th Street offered a serenade for him outside the archdiocese residence where he spent the night. The singers welcomed him to a new day with clear renditions of "Ode to Joy" and "You Are My Sunshine."

A torrent of nuns and priests moved past, some of them humming along, lining up for the Pope's morning prayer gathering at St. Patrick's Cathedral, next door.

"Hold it up!" a policeman named Dwyer shouted at one point as the line got too dense. Instantly dozens of nuns and priests raised their tickets to the service high in the air, then laughed at their error.

"Well, that's parochial education for you," one nun said.

Inside the cathedral, the congregation of religious was buoyant at this meeting with their leader. A few of the nuns along the way, dressed modern style in conservative mufti, seemed to have had their hair done for the occasion. But what was more striking was the great number of sisters who wore their religious habits — almost as if, after the recent years of informalization, they deliberately had donned their uniforms to identify with the Pope.

In the aisles of the cathedral, the necessary staff mixing of entourage clerics and cautious but delighted police officials, seemed a marriage made in heaven.

"Can I have one of those Gaelic banners, father!" one Catholic policeman asked a priest-publicist on the papal tour.

Even a newsman couldn't resist the happy parochial mood.

"Do you know my brother — Father Stranahan?" an Associated Press man asked a Long Island priest.

The Pope's relaxed mood was evident early, as he entered the morning service in the cathedral, with crowds outside shouting "Long live the Pope!" He could be heard in playful response: "You are right."

After the morning prayers, the Pope's day moved rapidly, first downtown to see the teen-agers at Madison Square Garden, where he climbed once again into the "Popemobile," the white customized truck that trundles him through the arena. After lingering longer than his entourage wanted, he moved to the tip of Manhattan for the ceremony at the Battery.

There, he again lingered, sounding again the theme of human rights and making his reference to the city's Jewish population.

"Several common programs of study, mutual knowledge, a common determination to reject all form of anti-Semitism and discrimination, and various forms of collaboration for the human advancement, inspired by our common biblical heritage, have created deep and permanent links between Jews and Catholics," he said. "As one who in his homeland has shared the suffering of your brethren, I greet you with the word taken from the Hebrew language: Shalom. Peace be with you!"

It was one attempt in many that day to appeal to the different faces of New York. In departing from his final stop, at Shea Stadium, the Pope appealed in four languages — Polish, Italian, English and Spanish — to the city's polyglot heart, urging the inhabitants to be a city with a soul.

"And how do you do this?" he asked. "By loving each other."

Then Pope John Paul delivered a final blessing from his throne-like chair in the ball park and simply said "Goodbye" before he moved on to the next city.

MICHAEL DALY

The (New York) Daily News

Michael Daly was raised in Ireland, Chicago and New York. A graduate of Yale University, he has been a writer for the New York Daily News *since 1978. This is the first piece in a three-part series on three days in the frightened life of an elderly resident of Coney Island.*

JANUARY 23, 1979

Her flannel robe drawn tight at the waist, Jennie Kelly pads into the kitchen and takes down the 24 Budweiser cans stacked in front of the window.

"They're my burglar alarm," the 83-year-old widow tells you as she parts the blue cotton curtains, letting the early morning light creep into the room. Three inches of snow have fallen during the night, and a white shroud covers the vacant lot that sprawls below Jennie's window.

"Children," Jennie says, her breath clouding the glass. Two children, a girl in a blue parka and a boy wearing red rubber boots, dash into the lot. The boy scoops up two handfuls of snow as the girl ducks behind a pile of rubble and timber.

"Look out," Jennie says, laughing. For 20 minutes, she stands motionless by the window. This 2-by-3-foot sheet of glass is the closest Jennie Kelly gets to the world outside her apartment. It is 7:29 A.M., Saturday, Jan. 6, and Jennie Kelly is beginning the 119th day of her incarceration in a third-floor cell comprised of two rooms, each measuring 18 feet by 20 feet.

Unlike Rikers Island, there are no cellmates or exercise periods in Jennie's $98-a-month prison. There is only a radio, a window, and a nephew who visits once a week for ten minutes, leaving five tins of condensed milk, a box of tea, four cans of tuna, six carrots, five pounds of potatoes, two loaves of bread, a quart of tomato juice and a jar of raspberry jelly.

There are no bars on the window of the rooms in which Jennie serves a life sentence. The three locks on the door open from the inside. The walls that hold Jennie Kelly captive are made of fear — terror as real as brick and mortar.

Jennie ran into the first wall as she walked out of a grocery on Mermaid Avenue a year and a half ago.

"Hey, lady," a young voice shouted. As Jennie turned, a fist caught her in the stomach.

"I'm going to die," Jennie remembers thinking as she pitched forward onto the sidewalk. A boy who looked no more than 13 snatched her purse. Grabbing $11 from the change pocket, the boy tossed the pocketbook into the air. Gasping for breath, Jennie crawled across the wet concrete, feeling in the darkness for her personal papers, her makeup, and a roll of stamps. Jennie Kelly no longer went out after sundown.

Then, two months later, another boy, this one about 17, knocked her to the sidewalk on Surf Avenue. After taking her money, the boy squeezed both of Jennie's breasts, hard, his lips rolling back from his gritted teeth. Jennie Kelly was now cut off from her morning walk on the boardwalk.

Last September, the terror struck in Jennie's building. She heard the footsteps behind her just as she turned the key in the lock. A hand snaked around her neck and clamped over her mouth, the thumb digging into her right eye. A second hand pushed open the door. Slipping his left leg in front of her, the attacker hit her once, square in the back.

"The money," the attacker said. "Where is it?" Her cheek pressed against the floor, Jennie Kelly stared at the pair of blue sneakers. The right shoe went back, and Jennie closed her eyes, waiting for the blow she knew would crush her face. Instead, the toe dug in between the carpet and her nose, lifting her face.

"The money," the attacker said again.

"In the napkins," Jennie said, her hand raising from the floor and pointing toward the kitchen counter.

Folding her arms over her head, Jennie listened to the attacker tear through the apartment. Coat hangers scraped in the closet. Drawers tumbled to the floor. Clothing tore. A bottle of tranquilizers rattled in the bathroom. Finally, the door slammed, and Jennie Kelly heard feet pounding down the stairs.

"I had wet myself," Jennie now tells you as she stands by the kitchen window looking out at the snow. "I sat there wet and looked at the door and knew I would never go outside again. I knew I would not be brave enough to ever stand in that hallway alone again."

"Did you call the police?" you ask Jennie.

"No," Jennie says. "I was afraid. I have to live here after the police are gone."

"Why don't you move?" you ask her. Jennie walks to the bathroom door and points to the deep cast iron tub.

"After working, my husband soaked and smoked cigars and we talked," Jennie says, her fingers rubbing the edge of the tub. "That table you're sitting at is where we ate. I laugh sometimes when my nephew tells me I should move to a home, like this isn't my home. He means an old folks home. What, does your real home die before you do? The home he wants me to go to, I would wake up in the morning and know that after 84 years on this earth, all I had was what was hanging in the closet. That would kill me."

"What do you do for money?" Jennie is asked.

"I don't like to talk about my money," Jennie says. "It's private. I get my Social Security and the pension from my husband mailed right to the bank. My nephew uses it to pay rent and utilities. He doesn't charge me for the magazines he brings sometimes. It doesn't cost much to keep an old lady alive, and my husband when he died had worked all his life as a plumber and it worked out."

Walking into the kitchen, Jennie strikes a safety match and lights a stove burner. The spigot coughs and sputters as she fills the aluminum kettle.

"It sounds like me on a bad morning," Jennie says.

Like a priest preparing for Mass, carefully Jennie lines up a cup, a box of black tea, and a tin of Carnation milk. When the kettle whistles, she washes out the pot with the boiling water and measures out three even tablespoons of tea.

Dripping the milk slowly into the cup, Jennie watches the swirls of white mix with the tea. She brushes her hair back and holds her head an inch over the cup so the steam can roll up her cheeks.

"I do this sometimes and dream," Jennie says.

"What do you dream of?" Jennie is asked.

"People I knew, things I've done," Jennie says. "More memories I guess than dreams. Dreams are when you're young. Who dreams past 60? At 60, you have memories, at 60 you're old. And I've been old since 1955." Tipping the cup, Jennie lets a puddle of tea dribble into the saucer. Holding the cup in one hand, she blows on the saucer to cool the tea and lifts the plate to her lips.

"Delicious," she says. "I make delicious tea." Reaching across the white enameled table, Jennie flicks on the radio. A maintenance man, the newscaster said, had been stabbed to death in front of St. John's University in Queens. The Vietnamese were pressing on to Phnom Penh. Mayor Koch defended a $12 million raise for managerial staff.

"Things go on," Jennie says. Pouring a second cup of tea, Jennie recalls a hot afternoon on the beach at Coney Island in August 1951. Struck by a stomach cramp, a boy in the water called for help. Half the men on the beach dived into the surf. A man in blue and white trunks dragged the boy onto the sand and pumped his chest.

"Sometimes I feel like I'm drowning," Jennie says, moving to the window.

"What do you think would happen if you leaned out the window and shouted 'help'?" she is asked.

"Nothing," Jennie says. There was nothing done, Jennie tells you, when landlords started packing year-round welfare families into the nearby summer bungalows. There was nothing done when the fire started. There was nothing done when neighbors fled one after the other. There was nothing done when all but three of the 31 buildings on her block stood empty. For 33 of her 48 years in this apartment, Jennie tells you, Coney Island was "a working man's paradise." In the past 15 years, she says, parts of Coney Island have become a poor man's hell, where children prey on elderly women.

"Everybody knows about ladies like me," Jennie says. "Everybody knows and they just accept it. It is a jungle down here and I'm the weakest animal in the jungle. What can I do but hide?"

MARK BOWDEN

The (Baltimore) News American

Soon after his graduation from college in 1973, Mark Bowden became a feature writer for The (Baltimore) News American. *This selection is the introduction to a long piece on life in a Baltimore housing project. He is now science writer for* The Philadelphia Inquirer.

In the summer, when heat smothers the project, when huge clouds of dust drift up from construction on Route 40 next door into living rooms and bedrooms and kitchens, the people sometimes step up off their tiny porches, put one leg over the fencing and tumble down to die on the glass and garbage-strewn asphalt below.

They usually fall, say the people in the project, in the summer, when the heat whips their financial worries and family troubles and fears to a boil, when the accumulated outrages of being black and poor in the projects becomes too much. They fall or jump — sometimes they're pushed — when that last frightening step seems the easiest one to take.

Summertime ups The Beat, which is frantic anyway among the humanity jammed into 725 W. George Street, one of three 14-story low-income housing projects in a pocket of publicly sponsored ghettos off Pennsylvania Avenue. The kids boogie to The Beat and their mothers — most adults here are black women — just get winded. The Beat this summer is disco. It comes through the walls and floors through day and night . . . penetrates like a cotton bat — whump-whump-whump — to the brain . . . sometimes it seems to come from their bones. It is at once joyful and angry.

Helen Harrod has seen them fall. She doesn't like to think about it. She understands it. She is 38 and she has six children almost grown and two grandchildren and she has lived here — she shakes her head in disbelief when she says it — 13 years. The housing authority records say only two have fallen, but Helen remembers more.

Six floors up she counts on her fingers and strains to remember how many have dropped in that time, but she gives up. There was the woman on nine, and the one on 13, and the man they threw off four, the boy who fell from 14, and the baby who rolled right out of a bedroom window ... "I don't like to think about it," she says, and shudders.

She is a big woman. Her face still is smooth and youthful. Helen seems strong, anchorlike, but her nerves are bad. You can see it in her eyes: distrust, doubt, vulnerability. Her husband left her two years ago, and her oldest boy is in jail. Her oldest daughter has a 3-month-old baby girl and hasn't finished high school yet. Her doctor says she can't get a job because her nerves are bad, which makes her worry more. God knows what will happen next.

"I get this, I don't know, *dark* feeling over me," Helen says, folding her arms over her wide bosom protectively. "My heart pounds and the breaths come hard and fast and I gets scared. Ain't nothin' in particular scares me; I just gets scared. It's the fear; I can't get rid of it. I can't sleep. The last two times it happened I had to go to the hospital. I like to went crazy."

It happens most often in the summer because the children are out of school and she worries about them constantly. So when Helen talks about the people who jump she empathizes. She doesn't like to talk about it because she gets excited and then the feeling comes on.

"When they built this damn high-rise they ought to have fenced in these porches completely," she says.

"Wouldn't that make the project seem like a prison?" a visitor asks.

She leans forward in her chair smiling, amused suddenly, and reaches out to put one hand on his knee. "Honey, don't you know?" she says. "This *is* prison."

BILL LYON

The Philadelphia Inquirer

Bill Lyon, a sports columnist for The Philadelphia Inquirer, *has been a member of the staff since 1972. He has won 27 state and national writing awards. Before becoming a sports columnist in August 1973, he was business editor of the* Inquirer.

AUGUST 3, 1979

He was earthy and raw and profane and loving. He was a catcher and it was where he belonged, hunkered down in the dirt, scuffling in the dust, sweating honest sweat, jawing with umpires, cursing and cajoling his pitchers, never letting them give up because to him quitting was the most grievous of sins.

He played for the most glamorous team in sports, a fascinating collection of millionaires and egomaniacs, and he was their leader. It was a little like making the guy who stokes the blast furnace chairman of the board of a steel corporation. But it worked. They all listened to him.

The last time the Yankees had a captain he was Lou Gehrig, the man they called The Iron Horse. Almost 40 years went by, and a lot of players passed through that clubhouse enroute to bronze busts and Hall of Fame enshrinement but none was named captain. Not until Thurman Munson. And him they called Squatty Body.

He didn't object. He would have been uncomfortable with some heroic-sounding nickname anyway. Besides, he squirmed around pomposity and had no use for frills and facades.

"Ahhhh, I'm just a little fat guy," he would say. Thurman Munson harbored no self-delusions. He knew what he saw looking back at him from a mirror, and never pretended to be anything else.

When he was named captain, he growled his objections. He said he had a temper and was always cussing out people and sometimes became consumed by his own competitive fires. He was right about that. But he was wrong about thinking he would make a lousy leader. The players followed him because they respected him, and they respected him because he was, in the parlance of the streets, "up front." Thurman Munson blew no smoke. What others passed off as diplomacy and tact, he saw as con and duplicity.

"When you got to know him," said Jay Johnstone, the ex-Phillie, ex-Yankee, "he either liked you or he didn't like you. There was no in-between. But you always knew where you stood with him. He didn't talk out of both sides of his face."

A man could do a lot worse than that for an epitaph.

If there are writers who speak glowingly of Thurman Munson, they will hear thunder in the sky. It will be Thurman Munson objecting. "Tell the truth, you phony," he will rumble.

Because he did not get along well with the media. That should not be taken as a weakness on his part.

But he wasn't a sham about it. In *The Book of Sports Lists,* there is a section entitled "Thurman Munson's Ten Favorite Sportswriters." There follow ten blanks.

Most of his feud with the media stemmed from a magazine article in which it was claimed that Munson was peeved because he came out second best in an ego clash with Reggie Jackson.

"No matter what I said, it always came out the same way," he said, "and as long as that was the way it was going to be, as long as it came out controversial no matter what I said, I just shut up."

And so he did. He withdrew into a cocoon of silence. In retrospect, it probably was a wise retreat. He was in a nowin situation, anyway, and he was sharp enough to realize that to continue speaking would only further disrupt a team whose harmony was fragile at best. So he bit the bullet, and his tongue. It required a swallowing of his own ego to do so. That he did says much about him as a man.

He grew up in Ohio, went to Kent State. That's Cleveland Indians' territory. But Munson pulled for the Yankees. Partly out of perverse admiration.

"Everybody out there hated the Yankees," he explained, "so I rooted for 'em. They were cocky and I like a cocky athlete."

The Yankees made the mouthy kid from Ohio their first choice in the June '68 draft. He only played in 99 minor-league games before he was brought up at the end of

1969. Since 1970, the Yankees have never had another catcher.

His first 30 times at bat in the bigs, in his first full season, he got exactly one hit. He went into a moody, depressive funk. He could be snarly mean but he also had a lot of gravel in his gut. He ended the season, despite that horrendous start, hitting .302 and he was Rookie of the Year.

Of his exploits as a player, you will read more elsewhere. About how he hit .300 five times, about how he drove in 100 runs, about how he won three Gold Gloves, about his quick throwing release, his shoulder miseries, his clutch hitting.

But these are statistics, cold and without emotion, and they do not tell you of the fiber of the man. His strength was in his handling of pitchers, which in itself is an exercise in psychology. He cut through all of the pretense and the delays.

"If you ain't got it, then give the ball the hell up and get outta here. Don't say you got something left if you haven't. Be a martyr and we all lose," he would tell a pitcher who balked at admitting he had run out of stamina.

He knew how to manipulate each one, how to squeeze out the last juices of competitiveness in them, how to sweet-talk the guy who was being gnawed by self-doubt, coaxing him with that lumpy grin, and how to rev up the guy who was fighting the dog in him, fixing him with that cold stare that questioned the very core of the guy's manhood.

There was one side of Thurman Munson that the fans didn't see. He was a big family man. So much so that for years he had asked to be traded to the Indians. They are not a good team, nor have they been. Playing in Cleveland would have meant no playoffs, no World Series checks. But it would have meant playing close to home and that mattered more to him than anything else.

But, ironically, he was the only home-grown Yankee of the eight regulars. All the rest had been bought up in the flesh market somewhere else. Perhaps it was appropriate that he was a Yankee because there was in his gruff, grumpy manner a lot of streets of New York. The people there like their heroes to be mean and nasty because that is the only way you survive in that town. So they embraced him. They loved his stubby, scarred body, the way he played hurt and asked for neither mercy nor forgiveness, the way he bumped into umpires and blocked the plate. There wasn't any sleek Madison Avenue polish to Thurman Munson. He was blunt and direct and if you didn't like that, tough.

Athletes have a term for players who gut it out, who are out there when they should be in bed, who can perform under pressure, who don't disappear when it's time for sweaty palms. They call them "gamers." It means they'll be there, when it starts and when it ends, no matter what happens in between. A gamer is the guy you want up against your back when it's midnight in a back alley.

Thurman Munson was a gamer.

W.D. (ZEKE) WIGGLESWORTH

The Minneapolis Star

W.D. (Zeke) Wigglesworth was born in Colorado, but attended high school in Iran. He came to The Minneapolis Star *in 1971 and has reported from all over the world. This selection is the first part of his portrait of an old boom town, Tenstrike, Minn.*

SEPTEMBER 19, 1979

TENSTRIKE, Minn. — Not too long after the railroad came through here, back around the turn of the century, the place was crawling with merchants and lumber barons and the other trappings of a lumber camp outgrowing its britches.

If you can believe local legends, there were 13 hotels and 13 whorehouses, and when the lumberjacks came into town in the spring with a winter's pay in their pokes, downtown Tenstrike looked like Dodge City after a cattle drive.

The legends are probably a bit skewed toward the colorful, but in truth, the place was prosperous and did have at least two hotels. Exact tallies on the ratio of pleasure palaces to hotels apparently have not been kept. But there was a doctor here, and a lawyer, and a blacksmith, and prosperity was on the wind.

Between then and now, the town burned down at least twice, got moved at least once, the timber stands were cleared and the hotels faded back into the landscape, taking the lumberjacks and the fallen doves with them.

On this chilly Friday morning, what's left of Tenstrike is quiet. The northwest wind skitters across Gull Lake, rattles the reeds, twirls the empty floating soft drink cans bobbing in the foam at the lakeshore, wisps up the hill across U.S. Highway 71, slips over the buried foundations of old buildings and stirs the flowers in Grandma Fellows' side yard.

A block away from Grandma's house, next to Mel's Place and kitty-corner from the Tenstrike Bar and Steakhouse, a black pup sits on a small knoll of grass and gnaws a bone. The left ear is straight up, the right ear is laid down. When the critter barks, both ears go straight back. The dog loves to bark at strangers.

Mel's is on the corner, painted in the colors chosen to decorate many a gym for the Class of 1958 senior prom: charcoal gray and pink. Between the dog and Mel's is the Tenstrike City Hall, used once a month for village meetings. The shades are drawn, the door is locked.

Down from the Tenstrike Bar, a right turn, then a left, is the empty and vandalized Lutheran church, flanked by two old fir trees and perched in the middle of an unmown stand of grass. Little chips of stained glass are stuck in the battered sashes of the gaping windows, and the inside walls are covered with pornographic graffiti.

The white-painted wooden altar is stuck back into the apse, with two crushed Pepsi cans on its top. One of the double doors at the church entrance has been broken off and is lying at an angle on the concrete front steps. Patches of green moss grow on the north side of the wooden-shingle steeple. The huge boiler sits in the basement, surrounded by crumpled concrete and scattered debris. The cornerstone says the church was built in 1921. A hundred yards away, glistening white in the sun, is the new community church, white siding and a tall white steeple, neat gravel parking lot.

Some of the 138 or so folks in Tenstrike are ashamed of the church, what has happened to it, the vandalism and the decay, and would like to tear it down and use the land for a park. But it belongs to a man who lives out of town, and he refuses to tear it down, according to the villagers, because he says it's a house of the Lord.

About the only sounds coming from Tenstrike today, aside from the yips of the loudmouthed pooch next to city hall, are occasional bumps and thuds and motor noises coming from the village's only industry, the Land O Lakes Wood Preserving Co. The yard, which chemically treats fence posts and construction lumber, is run by Babe Fellows, one of Grandma's three sons. It processed a million board feet last year, but the pace around the yard is slow and quiet. One of the workers, a kid from Fort Myers, Fla., is working in the chilly wind in his shirt-sleeves. "Love the country," he says. "Beats the hell out of Florida."

It's high noon now, and Ron Brasseur turns on the neon signs of the Tenstrike Bar. One of the signs says 'Information.' The bar sits right on what used to be the main highway to Blackduck, now just a paved bypass with no traffic. The information sign is a holdover from those days, and Brasseur says nobody much pays attention to it.

The Tenstrike is a lot bigger than Mel's. It has a dining room (where Gerry, Ron's wife, serves up nummy steaks), and a dance floor and a big bar. It also has one of the classiest jukeboxes in The Outback. Everything from the Sons of the Pioneers to Cannonball Adderly to the Bee Gees. "Cool Water" drifts through the darkness of the bar, which at the moment is low on clientele. Up on a mirror behind the bar is a red bumper sticker: TENSTRIKE, MINN. WHERE EVERYDAY IS A HOLIDAY.

BARRY BEARAK

The Miami Herald

Barry Bearak has been a Miami Herald *staff writer since 1976. He joined the* Herald *as a sportswriter and began writing news and features a year later. He has reported extensively on Florida's death penalty and covered Hurricanes David and Frederic. This piece concerns a murder in the south Miami area.*

JULY 15, 1979

It was one of those excuse-me killings, a scared hooker caught in a crossfire between two toughs. One had a .22 and shot from a crouch. The other used a .38, fired from his moving LTD. One had hustled the other out of 25 cents in a crap game.

Betsy Mae Little, 23, dies face up on SW 220th Street. She had a fine figure, charged $10 a go, $20 for whites. She was good people, not much trouble, a lady who'd occasionally whisper a secret or two to the cops.

She had started her dash for cover from The Storeporch, a decrepit row of bars and shops. It's the hangout where Betsy Mae Little grew up, the hangout where she worked. Her best friends saw her killed there under the noontime sun.

A month later, assistant state attorney Jeff Raffle said he hated the case. "Fifty people saw it," he griped. "The day it goes down, there's lots of hollering. When it comes time to take statements — magic — everything gets quiet."

Fifty witnesses. And no witnesses.

Raffle gave the case to Metro investigator Rich Bolin, a balding man who's been around a long time. "Storeporch," he said. "We ain't worth a damn in that part of town."

It is poor. It is black. And The Storeporch, the hub, is a dingy magnet in a gloomy pocket of Goulds. A half block west of U.S. 1 on 220th, it is tucked between weeds, broken glass and railroad tracks.

Thirty-five years ago, it was just a grocery in a Jim Crow slum. Black migrants waited outside for trucks to take them into the fields. The trucks no longer come: the people still do. Since 1965, there have been other stores added. Now the grocery is a pool hall, and its neighbors are a barber shop, a dry goods store and bars.

Out front sits the porch, holy wood to three generations. Old-timers lean on its posts, hide their desolation in the mists of memory and the taste of cheap wine. The young suck spirit from aluminum cans and hand-rolled cigarets. Comfort sometimes rushes through a needle, and trouble comes as quickly as a roll of the dice.

Rich Bolin drove up last week in a white Toyota. He wore a blue polyester leisure suit, his gun in a belt under the jacket. He looked like a cop.

Most on the porch withheld any subtlety from their stares. A few scattered. Money disappeared into pockets. Bags of white powder were slipped into the weeds.

"I'm looking for Myrtice Lovett," Bolin, 55, said to a young woman in the pool hall.

"Who?" she said. "You crazy. Nobody here like that."

"Myrtice Lovett," he repeated. "She works here."

"Ain't seen Myrtice Lovett for months."

Myrtice Lovett is Bolin's witness. She gave a statement to police the day of the murder, June 11. It is a blurry account, short on facts. She said the only shots she heard came from the .22 pistol of Harry (Ski-bow) Damen, a Storeporch regular with a short fuse and a long rap sheet.

Ski-bow, 28 is in jail, charged with Murder One. The fatal bullet was a .22. Still, the case stinks. Ski-bow and his brother-in-law, Willie Lockhart, swear that he only returned fire at the passing car. It is a swearing contest.

Bolin crossed the street, walked toward Betty and Bob's Soul Bar. "I don't see nothing," he joked to the men playing craps on a piece of plywood next to the building. He opened the screen door.

Inside, he started to chat. People pointed him to a shoeless, shirtless man who was counting his tricks in a game of bid whist. Bob Fagan nodded, led the investigator to the far end of his hot, grimy bar where he stacks paint cans and mattresses. It was Bolin's first break.

"Like I say, I really didn't see it," Fagan, 58, said slowly. "And I really wouldn't want to say anything about something I didn't see."

Bolin parried, "I know, and folks don't want to lose a lot of work days testifying before a bunch of tricky lawyers."

"A lot of colored people's afraid," Fagan agreed. "They feel if Ski-bow gets out, he comes looking for them."

The talk was obtuse. But it was friendly.

For 90 minutes, Bolin bought the beers and tried to butter up a possible source. He talked about the smooth taste of moonshine, told murder stories, mentioned mutual acquaintances. Occasionally, he'd edge back to the subject.

"Without cooperation, this place could turn into a jungle," he'd say; Bob Fagan would tilt his head.

Outside, on The Storeporch, people wondered what was going on inside Bob's. They don't like trouble, no matter who brings it. They don't like the heroin trade in front of Johnny's Lounge. They don't like the ripoffs and the fistfights and the times when people with guns in their pockets go crazy on the booze or the dope.

Nor do they like the do-gooders from the east side of the tracks who say The Storeporch ought to go. It is their place. Some people go to movies; they go to The Storeporch.

And most don't like cops. There are several hundred arrests made at Storeporch each year, police say. It's one of South Dade's biggest trouble spots. It's hot, there's action, there are problems. Some people cooperate; some don't.

"I'm not asking anyone to fink on anybody for Chrissake," Rich Bolin pitched. "We know who did the shooting."

Bob Fagan sipped his Miller's.

He softened.

"A whole heap of 'em seen it," he said. "You ain't got to worry. I'll get you someone who see'd it, no pretender."

He did.

He introduced Bolin to James Tucker, an old man in a straw hat. Tucker said he'd seen it all. Bolin cracked a smile.

"They call you Red, don't they?" Bolin buddied up to his new friend.

"Some call me Red, some call me J.D.," Tucker replied. He let the investigator treat him to a pint of Thunderbird.

The next day Bolin picked up Tucker and took him downtown. Prosecutor Raffle asked questions. The old-timer talked. A stenographer took it down.

Ski-bow Damon goes on trial Aug. 27.

Maybe.

"It's looking worse all the time," Raffle says. "The old man has one eye. His story is confusing. It helps us; it hurts us."

Each day Rich Bolin returns to Goulds.

"There are more witnesses out there," he says. "A whole porch full."

MARTIN BERNHEIMER

Los Angeles Times

Born in Munich, Germany, Martin Bernheimer came to the Los Angeles Times *as music critic with wide experience in music, criticism and teaching. This selection is his introduction to a long piece on a British music festival.*

JULY 22, 1979

LEWES, Sussex — "If you're going to spend all that money, John, for God's sake do the thing properly."

The words were spoken some 45 years ago. John was John Christie, a very rich, very British gentlemen who also happened to be a physicist. The speaker was Audrey Mildmay, a young soprano who had recently become Mrs. Christie. The thing was Glyndebourne.

To anyone not indoctrinated in the peculiar ways of elitism and the arts, all that may take a little explaining.

Christie owned a gorgeous estate in Sussex, 55 miles from London. It was, and is, a sprawling Tudor wonder, an elegant manor surrounded by graceful slopes inhabited by the most docile of cows and sheep. Christie, an artistic dabbler, wanted to build a tiny opera house on the estate as a gift to his bride. He toyed with putting on some intimate Wagner and, even curiouser, contemplated installing a pit that would accommodate only a few strings and an electric organ.

Miss Mildmay, sensible even when dealing with preposterous dreams, persuaded her husband to substitute Mozart for Wagner, and to create a performance enterprise that would not allow compromises. Christie responded accordingly.

He set out to give England and his wife a unique festival, one that could stand easy comparison, in its special way, with Munich and Salzburg. Rehearsals would be virtually unlimited. Staging would be sensitively detailed. The dramatic credibility gap would be minimized. The best possible singers, directors and conductors would be invited to participate, not for huge fees but for the pleasure, and stimulation, of working under virtually ideal, controlled artistic conditions.

Christie, who cherished the quixotic challenge, aimed instantly for "Not the best we can do but the best that can be done anywhere."

He enlisted no less a musician than Fritz Busch, no less a man of the theater than Carl Ebert. (Years later, Ebert would be frustrated in his own dream of nurturing a Glyndebourne, of sorts, in Los Angeles). During its first festival fortnight in 1934, Glyndebourne played Mozart only, and the house had a seating capacity of 300.

Like everything else, Glyndebourne has changed and grown over the years. But not too much.

Christie and his wife are now dead, but their son, George, carries on in the established tradition, with Moran Caplat as general administrator (one Rudolf Bing used to have that job). Bernard Haitink is the current music director and John Cox supervises the staging. The theater has been enlarged — if that is the word — to the point where it can accommodate 800 lucky operagoers. Private industry has begun to help subsidize the festival, and the British government contributes to the support of a touring company which carries the Glyndebourne message to various provincial centers after the season proper has ended. The touring ensemble comprises young British singers who serve, for the most part, as understudies during the gala festival.

The thing has been done properly.

PAUL GALLOWAY

Chicago Sun-Times

Paul Galloway, a reporter for the Chicago Sun-Times *since 1969, wrote a series of stories from a Cambodian refugee camp, one of which is reprinted below. He is the co-author of* Bagtime, *a fictional account of "the joys and perils of Chicago life."*

DECEMBER 12, 1979

SAKEO, Thailand — This is a hellhole of a camp. There are 30,000 Cambodian refugees existing within the barbed wire that circles a compound of 40 acres. Officials here figure that each person has two square meters of living space.

There are only a few trees, and they are stunted, gnarled and offer no shade. The sun is ruthless today. It is easily 95 degrees.

Sewage runs in ditches only inches away from deplorable huts, no larger than rabbit hutches, where people — families — live. The stench is, as you would imagine, oppressive. Here, at Sakeo (sah KAY oh), you are grateful for the pervasive smoke from the wood fires. It helps to cut the odor of excrement and urine.

The military presence is conspicuous. Armed guards, who will shoot to kill escapees, surround the camp, which bears this sign at its entrance: Illegal Immigrants Centre.

The trails inside are clotted with refugees. Many more closely resemble clumps of filthy, black rags than human beings. You are struck by the number of men and boys, some with a leg missing, on crutches.

It is difficult to report dispassionately on such a scene.

If measures seem harsher here, it is because of the inhabitants. Inmates, surely, is a more accurate word.

These are the survivors of a Vietnamese army offensive in late October against a Khmer Rouge guerrilla detachment. More than 30,000 people, most of the Cambodian refugees encamped in a settlement on the Cambodian frontier, were pushed into Thailand by the attack.

It is a familiar story: civilians fleeing hunger and war, being dominated by guerrilla bands fighting the Vietnamese invaders. In this case, the oppressors are the communist Khmer Rouge.

These people will be here a long time, even the women and children, because everyone has been labeled Khmer Rouge. It is easy to identify the guerrillas, however. They are healthier, better fed than the ordinary refugees.

Images that stay with you: A small girl, perhaps six years old, rolls the top of a straw basket in the dust. It topples over. She rolls it again. Then she stares at you. She does not smile.

A boy comes to your side. He is about eight years old. His blue shirt is soaked with sweat. He smiles, and you find yourself saying, "You'll be fine, kid." You know better.

Bob Beck, a physician who is treating the Sakeo refugees as a volunteer for the World Relief Commission, paused to talk about the camp: "These people were driven out by the Vietnamese, who cut the Khmer Rouge supply route. Most are victims of circumstance.

"I have an interpreter who sometimes talks about what it was like in Cambodia. I can't comprehend it. He was a schoolteacher. He changed his name and survived. He had a friend who worked hard in the fields. One day, the soldiers learned (his friend) had been a teacher, and they shot him to death."

Beck told of a woman here who had lost a child to malnutrition: "Her husband was a Khmer Serel. The Rouge murdered him. She's afraid for her life. I'm keeping her in the hospital for protection.

"There is a festering hostility here. The overcrowding, the sheer boredom will be trouble. But most are nonpolitical and are disillusioned with the Khmer Rouge."

If ever a piece of hell needed a guardian angel, Sakeo does. It may be an exaggeration to say that it has one. She is at least a saint.

Her name is Eva den Hartog. She is 57 years old, a major in the Salvation Army and she has been helping the desperate for the last 20 years, in Bangladesh, in Africa, all over the world.

"When I came here in October, it was bad," she said. "We had 50 to 55 deaths each day. Yesterday, there was one death. I don't know how many today. It has been better. Two deaths one day. Five the next. Six the next. Then one. It's wonderful what can be done."

She has short, auburn hair, thick glasses, freckled arms. She is wearing a short-sleeved, white tunic with a Salvation Army pin on each lapel.

"The stench is unbearable, but they are preparing running water and electricity," she said. "They have enough food now and good medical care. You can't get better medicine in Europe. Of course, this is not a European hospital."

She sits down for a moment. She arrived here Oct. 24, and she has not taken a day off. There is a sign tacked to the wall behind her. It says, "Be still and know that I am God."

Den Hartog, who is Dutch and now assigned to California, is in charge of medical treatment here as director of the Christian Medical Team, which is sponsored by five Christian organizations.

"It's tragic," she said. "These people are innocent victims of a dirty political system. What I saw when I came here was a wretched, stinking, starving flotsam of a population.

"We say there are no slaves anymore. I say there are millions of slaves like these people without the name.

"I am proud I can take care of them. It doesn't matter who they are or what they believe. I want to help the suffering, and this is one of the biggest tragedies in world history. It is a disgrace to the human race."

Seeing all this, doesn't she sometimes question her faith?

"I must be honest with you," she said. "I have moments when I cannot reconcile what I see with my belief in a loving God. I think, 'God does not care!'

"But on the other hand, God has put me here. I know what I must do. I am His hands and feet and lips. I am an ordinary woman, but I can help. When I have doubts, I say God will look past my limitations. The apostle Paul said, 'I can do all things through Christ.' I believe that.

"I have seen a lot in my life. I have seen 150 deaths in one day. I have become a woman with strong convictions.

"I know there is a power behind me that no one can take away from me. As long as we're moved by compassion, if we can say, 'This could be my mother, my father,' then we can do the job.

"Christians must be practical. The slogan of the Salvation Army is Soup, Soap, Salvation. First things first. And we have come so far at Sakeo.

"In the beginning, no child would smile. Now they are smiling. And that is wonderful."

Cover, vignettes and design by Diane Tonelli

Illustrations on pages 9, 18, 26, 37, 47, 71, 78, 89, 98, 109, 129, 133 and 139 by Joe Tonelli